NATIONAL
THEATRE
PLAYS

STATE OF REVOLUTION

STATE
OF REVOLUTION

A Play in Two Acts
by

ROBERT BOLT

HEINEMANN
in association with the National Theatre
LONDON

Heinemann Educational Books Ltd
LONDON EDINBURGH MELBOURNE AUCKLAND TORONTO
HONG KONG SINGAPORE KUALA LUMPUR NEW DELHI
NAIROBI JOHANNESBURG LUSAKA IBADAN
KINGSTON

ISBN
0 435 23131 6 (paper)
0 435 23130 8 (cased)

Published by
Heinemann Educational Books Ltd
48 Charles Street, London W1X 8AH
Set in 10/11pt Garamond by
Spectrum Typesetting, London
and printed in Great Britain by
Biddles Ltd, Guildford, Surrey

INTRODUCTION

Stalin's modernization of Russia was a material achievement which transcends the achievement of Peter the Great. But the price which Russia paid for it was dreadful. This was admitted by Kruschev at the Twentieth Party Congress in 1956. Stalin's evil practices were much mitigated at the time. But little if anything was done either to inhibit the machine or reconsider the philosophy which had made his practice possible. This is all the more depressing because in that philosophy it is not the possible which happens but the probable.

In Marx's view, History very largely goes the way it must. It is the nature of society which decides the nature of events. Great men are men with great qualities certainly, but those qualities lie dormant unless they are apposite to the social situation. Great men don't make History; History finds the men it needs. If Napoleon had died in childhood a sufficiently similar man would have played the part which Napoleon played. There was only one Napoleon because History only needed one, not because the man was matchless. Individual heroes and heroines appear to cause events because they are in some way individually striking and conspicuously situated but the events which they appear to cause are actually caused by social forces which no individual can possibly control. A man, however greatly gifted, who attempts to impose his will upon a situation which does not require him will be brushed aside as a sparrow by a locomotive. The greatest revolutionary leader cannot make his greatness actual until there is a revolutionary situation. A potential dictator remains potential unless the situation is ripe for dictatorship. It is the nature of society which determines what we do, not the other way round. Kruschev denounced Stalin for the "Cult of Personality". Stalin had credited himself with a degree of influence which according to Marx it is impossible that any individual should exercise. Hence, said Kruschev, the Stalinist tyranny. Since Stalin was now dead, Stalinist tyranny also was dead. But that was to say that the course of events and the nature of Soviet society *had* resulted from Stalin's influence. Which is the cult of personality.

He also denounced Stalin for violating "revolutionary legality". There is in Marxism no such thing. "The revolutionary dictatorship of the proletariat" said Lenin, "is rule won and maintained by the use of violence . . . rule that is unrestricted by any laws". Felix Dzerzhinsky, the revered and puritanic founding-father of the Cheka, was even less equivocal about revolutionary legality. "To us" he said quite simply "all things are permitted". These startling statements were not made off the cuff; they have deep philosophic roots in Marxism itself.

In Marx's view there can be no such thing as a universal human ethic so long as there are social classes. There can only be the different ethics of the different classes which are tailored to their social needs. Man is a social animal. He associated first in order to survive and then in order to produce. Production is the driving force in all societies. In all societies a class which owns the means of production exploits the labour of a class which doesn't. The ideology and institutions of all societies reflect this economic base. The ideology includes the ethic which claims to be a universal human ethic but is in fact the ethic of the ruling class. And the laws which codify the ethic are the laws of the ruling class. And the State which enforces the laws is an instrument of the ruling class. And all class rule, however well disguised, and even self-deceived, is dictatorial.

So what is the ethic of the revolution? Lenin is unequivocal about this too. "We say that our morality is entirely subordinated to the interests of the class struggle of the proletariat . . . We say: morality is what serves to destroy the old exploiting society and to unite all the toilers around the proletariat, which is creating a new communist society". In short, whatever conduces to the victory of the proletariat is

2

ipso facto morally good. Now if you base specific laws on an ethic such as that you may be morally compelled to break them. You cannot grant the legal right to anything specific because there may be circumstances under which anything specific may not conduce to victory.

All class struggles, Marx had said, were fierce and total. But the fight between the proletarian and capitalist classes would be the last and most worthwhile. For the outcome of the proletarian revolution was a classless society in which there would be neither need nor opportunity for the exploitation of one group by another. Lenin mistrusted too much speculation about the new society. Its details were unguessable and speculation diverted energy from the immediate programme, which was sternly practical and went like this:

The proletariat would establish itself by revolution as the new ruling class. Unlike other ruling classes it would be candid about that. It's rule would be openly and proudly dictatorial. The proletariat would seize the means of production. The proletarian State, that is, would seize the means of production. The State and the proletariat would be one and the same thing. (Marx says that plainly. He speaks of centralizing everything "in the hands of the State, i.e., of the proletariat organized as the ruling class".). The defeated bourgeoisie and their allies would put up a frantic rearguard resistance and this would have to be crushed without mercy. The first part of the revolution would then be accomplished. Then would come a longer but more peaceful struggle—the eradication of bourgeois thinking. When that was done, the State would vanish and the classless community appear. The State would vanish of itself; in the famous phrase it would "wither away" like any other useless organ. It would be useless because the only function of the State is the rule of one class over others. And classes are defined by ownership. So when everything was owned by everyone or if you like when nobody owned anything, everyone would be of the same class, which is to say that there would be no classes. Marx goes on about this at some length and has some vividly interesting things to say about human nature, its past and present limits and future possibilities. But that is the gist of his argument.

And that is the only argument which he advances against the obvious dangers of concentrating both economic and political power in the hands of a dictatorial State. He rejects for instance the idea of an independent judiciary to protect the citizen against the State; so long as there is a ruling class there can be no such thing as an independent judiciary. The claim of the State to be an impartial arbitrator raised above the warring classes is entirely spurious. He is contemptuous too of parliamentary rule by an elected majority; that can only (and at best) reflect the structure of a class society, it cannot alter it. The point is to abolish classes and so allow the community at large to swallow up the State. He does suggest a couple of safeguards which Lenin wanted to apply but dropped. Neither of them worked for fairly obvious reasons. They were: that State officials should enjoy no privilege but be paid the same as a skilled labourer, and that they should be subject to recall at short notice by those who elected them. But once a man has power, privilege descends upon him automatically. Others will impose it on him even if he doesn't want it. And as for recall, once he possesses power and privilege, who will venture to suggest it? A Soviet State official now can only be shifted by a higher official, and he enjoys a degree of privilege quite novel in its impudence. (That a man should be given a special car and a servant to save him the trouble of driving, that we are familiar with, but a special traffic-lane to drive it on is something never seen before). Apart from those two safeguards, which he offers more or less en passant in his account of the Paris Commune, Marx's argument remains as I have outlined it in the preceding paragraph.

It is an argument conducted in highly abstract terms. It uses the word "State" as though the State were an abstraction, instead of what it is. It equates the State first with the proletariat and then with the community. Again and again both Marx and Engels use "State", "proletariat", "society" as though they were interchangeable, which they are not.

The Party too is equated with the proletariat. It has, says Marx "no interests separate and apart from those of the proletariat as a whole". The only difference which he admits is not a difference but a claim to a special identity: The Party has "over the great mass of the proletariat the advantage of clearly understanding the line of march, the conditions, and the ultimate general results of the proletarian movement". It is the conscious essence of the proletariat. The proletariat has a role to play, imposed upon it by the laws of History. All proletarians have this role, aware of it or not. The laws of History are objective and inexorable. Those who are most aware of it constitute the Party. Thus the proletariat is the current instrument of History. And the Party is its consciousness.

This metaphysical strain in Marxism (which presumably derives from Hegel and the philosophical idealism in which the young Marx was saturated and became an adept) is rendered dangerous by the claim of Marxism to scientific status. And that claim is central. It is that which distinguishes Marxist socialism from moralistic, utopian socialism. Now a scientific truth is a truth which can be demonstrated; it is a fact, not a matter of opinion; until it can be demonstrated it remains an hypothesis. A metaphysical truth can't be demonstrated, it remains a matter of opinion. And a dictatorial Party which supposes its opinions to be demonstrable facts is a dangerous entity.

Marx's Party, the First International, was a broad organization, open to anybody of good will. Lenin's Bolshevik Party was open only to active revolutionaries willing to submit themselves to centralized discipline. Each unit of the Party was subordinate to the one above in a hierarchy culminating in the Politburo, a sort of revolutionary Cabinet drawn from the Central Committee. And Lenin's personal prestige was such that in a matter of any importance the Politburo never disagreed with him for any length of time. Thus the consciousness of the proletariat, which was the instrument of History, became the consciousness of a single man. In case you think I am exaggerating, here is Lenin himself: "That in the history of revolutionary movements the dictatorship of individuals was very often the expression, the vehicle, the channel of the dictatorship of the revolutionary classes has been shown by the irrefutable experience of history". It is certainly a fact that revolutions have often issued in dictatorship by individuals. But that the power of those individuals embodied in some way the power of whole classes is not a fact but an assertion, and one for which it would be hard to offer tangible proof. Again: "There is therefore absolutely no contradiction in principle between Soviet (that is socialist) democracy and the exercise of dictatorial powers by individuals". If dictatorship and democracy are not metaphysical concepts but actual systems of government then the contradiction between them is total, in Soviet Russia or anywhere else. Those systems are most dictatorial in which power is most concentrated and those are most democratic in which it is most spread. And you can no more spread by concentrating than you can heat by cooling or descend by going up. Everything no doubt is relative but Lenin goes out of his way (he always did) to talk "absolutely" and "in principle".

That there was in fact a contradiction was demonstrated shortly after the revolution. The Party encountered opposition not only from the remnants of the bourgeoisie from whom it was expected, and from the peasants, whose revolutionary consciousness had always been in doubt, but from less conscious sections of the proletariat itself.

Now that the factories were theirs, the workers wanted to run the factories. But worker control proved inefficient. This was a serious matter. Factory production, Lenin said, was "the material base and source of socialism". And factory production called for "absolute and strict unity of will". But that could only be ensured "by thousands subordinating their will to the will of one". Were the proletariat fully conscious the absolute authority which he now demanded for individual factory directors "would be something like the mild leadership of the conductor of an orchestra". But in the absence of such consciousness it might assume "sharp forms". Sharp forms, according to the Workers Opposition group which now sprang up in the Party itself, means the presence of the Cheka at factory meetings and the arrest of troublemakers from the factory floor. "Be that as it may" said Lenin "unquestioning obedience to a single will is absolutely necessary for the success of large-scale industry".

Reluctantly one must admit that he was probably right. Even in stable and prosperous times it is a puzzle to see how daily managerial decisions can be democratically arrived at by the thousands of workers who will carry them out. In the desperate times which followed on the War and Civil War in Russia is was patently impossible. But the workers didn't like it and now arose a second group within the Party, a Democratic Opposition, demanding the right to disagree. This was even worse than the Workers Opposition. If the Party should divide into consciously opposing factions, who could say which faction was the true material envelope of the disembodied consciousness of the proletariat itself? Lenin met this knotty problem in a crunchingly practical manner. Factions were forbidden.

This was done in 1921 at the Tenth Party Congress, which also met the problem presented by the peasants. But this problem was met by relaxing rather than increasing the requirements of the State. The peasant problem had its roots in the circumstances of the revolution in 1917. Until that date there had been only one serious attempt at proletarian revolution, in 1905, and that attempt though brilliantly and bravely led (by Trotsky) had been short-lived and never really looked like winning. Conditions were not ripe for it. The proletariat was a new and small minority. Nine Russians out of ten were peasants. Russia was still a semi-feudal country. There had been peasant risings big and small throughout her history. The programme of the peasant risings was always a straightforward demand for land, for the division among the peasants of the great estates belonging to the landowning nobility who battened cruelly on peasant labour. It was not a socialist programme; the peasant demanded land for himself and was ferociously proprietorial.

The peasant risings had always been put down by the Army. But the World War of 1914-18 was fought with conscript Armies. The peasant was put in uniform, given a gun and taught how to use it. The Russian armies suffered dreadfully, partly from the general backwardness of Russia, and partly from the irresponsibility and selfishness of the Russian aristocracy and the clumsy inefficiency of the Russian State bureaucracy. The Russian Army (and Navy) mutiny of 1917 was the last and greatest of the peasant risings and no army now could put it down because the peasants were themselves the Army.

7

Their demand was simple: Peace and Land.

The Tsar resigned his power to a bourgeois government which promulgated a Parliamentary constitution. In Marxist terms the feudal epoch came to an end and the epoch of bourgeois democracy started. But still the streets of Petrograd and Moscow milled with mutinous troops and militant factory workers. This was the situation which Lenin seized upon.

The other left-wing parties were frightened and bemused. The Essars who were traditionally the party of the peasants were willing to wait for the great estates to be divided up in an orderly way by legislation. The Mensheviks (a Marxist Party like the Bolsheviks and claiming to be revolutionary but in Lenin's view corrupted by reformist tendencies) pointed out that according to Marx the socialist revolution would only be successful in developed capitalist countries with large, developed proletariats. Any attempt at it in Russia must inevitably fail and lead to the triumph of bloody reaction. True, said Lenin, but the Russian revolution would only be a part — and that not the most significant part — of the European revolution. And Europe as a whole did have a large, developed proletariat. The Russian Revolution would be quickly followed by revolutions in Germany and France, and very likely in Britain too. The European proletariat would pour consumer goods and capital equipment into Russia from the cornucopia of their own developed industries and thus secure the triumph of the Russian proletariat too. This was not political sophistry. A reading of his statements shows that he was perfectly serious. If it didn't happen he said the Russian revolution was doomed and would go down in history as a mere rehearsal for the real thing. But it was bound to happen. Marx had said repeatedly that revolutions were most likely in the most developed countries. If Russia was ripe for revolution — and it clearly was — those more developed countries must be yet more ripe.

The other difficulty pleaded by the Mensheviks (and by most of the Essars and Bolsheviks too) was this: The trenches were deserted and the German Armies were advancing over Russia unopposed. Quite apart from patriotic duty, the German Kaiser would put the clock back if he conquered, would reinstate the Tsar. German conquest would be counter-revolution. Therefore it was their revolutionary duty to resist him. Lenin dismissed this. In the first place, if they asked the troops to return to the trenches they wouldn't go. And in the second place if they did return to the trenches they would return to the command of the officer caste and the bourgeois government. And *that* would be counter-revolution.

As the chaos mounted, the mood of the masses became desperate. They were ready for anything, ready with firm leadership to make another revolution. This proved to be true. The Bolsheviks offered leadership, the masses accepted it and made the October revolution which carried them to power. The Bolsheviks had articulated their demands. The proletarian demand was socialism out and out. The peasant demand as we have seen was seizure of the land but not by any means socialism. Trotsky (who prepared and organized the actual coup) admits frankly in his History of the Revolution that the Party deliberately misled the peasants about this. The peasants were encouraged to suppose that by "seizing the land" the Bolsheviks meant what the peasants meant. The peasants, as Trotsky says, would not have been interested in State ownership. After the revolution this dangerous misunderstanding remained to be cleared up. All land was declared to be State property, but that decree was written in the air of Petrograd. The peasant had the land and regarded it as his.

This brings us back to 1921 and the Tenth Party Congress. A lenient solution to the peasant question was strongly suggested by the tragedy of the Kronstadt rising which overshadowed the proceedings. The rising was bloodily put down by the Red Army which was urged into the battle by delegates who left the Congress for that purpose. But the remaining delegates could hear the guns and we are told that the sound depressed them.

The Kronstadt sailors, the erstwhile "flower and pride of the revolution" had demanded among others things an end to what they called the "terrorizing" of the peasants. This was a perjorative and hurtful term for something that was necessary. In the chaotic conditions then prevailing, the towns were literally starving. The countryside was hit less hard. Peasant holdings worked by hand can be worked under almost any conditions. There was grain in the countryside. But the peasants wouldn't part with it because although they were offered money for it, the factories were producing nothing which the money would buy. So the grain was simply taken from them. Some of the grain procurement squads had shown excessive zeal. Sometimes, Lenin said, two or three times the stipulated quantity was taken and the peasants themselves were left to starve. As we have seen, the majority of Russians were peasants and the proletariat itself was restive. By 1921 the Party was confronted by a sullenly indifferent or hostile population. Lenin responded with the New Economic Policy.

The State would continue to take some grain from the peasants but in small and specified quantities, as a tax in kind. The bulk of his harvest the peasant could sell on the open market. In short he would operate his holding, though it still belonged to the State, exactly as though it belonged to himself. Light industry and trading too would be conducted by individual entrepreneurs, operating at a profit. This was a return to capitalistic private enterprise which few but Lenin would have dared to advocate and none but Lenin could have carried. True, the land still legally belonged to the State, but the peasant had the actual possession of it. Marx-Leninists have scant respect for legal forms. It is the economic actuality which determines everything else. Would not this massive retreat towards a capitalist economy inevitably lead to the return of bourgeois social forms? No, said Lenin, not inevitably. The weapons of the State were now in the hands of the Party. They must be sharpened and used with double vigour. Meanwhile the peasants must be brought to collective farming "by persuasion and example".

That was the situation which Lenin left to his successors when he died in 1924. Their task was to build socialism. The very foundation of socialism was that the means of production should be in the hands of the State. The principle means of production in Russia was land. And the land was held by the peasants. Socialism also necessitated (for both Marx and Lenin) the sort of developed industry to be found in the advanced capitalist countries but not yet in Russia. From where could Russia get a surplus to invest in factories, mines and dams? Only from her agriculture. And the peasants were not willing to provide a surplus to invest in factories, mines and dams. What little they knew of Socialism did not attract them. The Party found itself hemmed in by this closed circle. But it had in its hands the sharpened and accumulating weapons of the dictatorial State. It had an arsenal of lethal language too, a tradition of violence and a theory which sanctified it.

Before the revolution the socialist State had been a dangerously flexible philosophic concept. By the time of Lenin's death it was a dangerously tangible and rigid apparatus. And Lenin had put it in Stalin's hands. Perhaps he hadn't realized quite what he was doing. Perhaps for him the socalist State remained a philosophic concept until, too late, the evidence of he senses forced him to a reappraisal; but a Marxist reappraisal would have meant a reappraisal of all that he had done. In his famous "Testament" he urges the Party to get rid of Stalin on the grounds that Stalin is too crude. This, Lenin is forced to admit "may seem to be a trifle". By Marxist criteria it is a trifle and a personal trifle at that. But Lenin the man goes on "it is a trifle which may come to be decisively significant". It did. But to a Marxist there can be no such thing as a decisively significant personal trifle. He warns the Party against a split. Such a split is possible he says because the Party's class support is split between the peasants and the proletariat. Good Marxism so far. "But" he goes on "a good half of the danger lies in the personal relations between Trotsky and Stalin". The relationship between two classes is thus asserted to be no more important than the relationship between two persons. That is not good Marxism. The Comrades shook their heads over this melancholy document, the work after all of a dying man, and decided to suppress it.

Quite soon after Lenin's death Stalin realized that Trotsky was objectively a counter-revolutionary. Trotsky wrote from exile that not he but Stalin was objectively a counter-revolutionary. But Stalin made his statement as the leader of the Party, and the Party ought to know. Was it not the consciousness and vanguard of the revolutionary proletariat? Trotsky was reluctantly forced to the conclusion that it was no longer so. His own tiny Party would take on that function. He seems to have learned nothing from all that he had been through.

He uses Marxist terminology in his account of Stalin's tyranny but that is all he does. And his disciples nowadays follow his lead. By following Trotsky into exile as it were they escape the intellectual responsibility for all that ensued. Stalin's tyranny is dealt with by calling it "the Soviet Thermidor*" likening it to the bourgeois reaction which overthrew Robespierre. And the degeneration of the Socialist State into something so sadly like any other state, with an arrogant bureaucracy pursuing selfish ends they deal with by pronouncing it a classically dialectical "Return of the Old in the New". But that is merely a pretentious way of saying something much more simply said without the benefit of Marx: that human selfishness is not so easily got rid of. Nor does it explain why what returned in the New was what was bad in the Old. Of course if you take Marx at his literal word, there could be nothing good in the old State. He says, and Engels and Lenin reiterate, that the bourgeois State is an instrument of class dictatorship and nothing else but that. But this is patent nonsense. It may be mainly that, but there is an obvious difference between living in a capitalist democracy like (say) Britain and living in a capitalist fascist State like (at the time of writing) Chile. The difference between living where a policeman must show you a warrant before he may enter your house and living where the police may snatch you on your way to work and leave your body on a rubbish-dump is material and beneficent.

The comparison with Thermidor seems to me a bad one. And it wouldn't help the case even if it were a good one. The fact that something has happened before doesn't explain why it happened again nor tell you how it might have been avoided. The economic and class forces which produced the Thermidor of 1794 are obvious to any Marxist. Trotsky doesn't specify the forces which produced the Soviet Thermidor of 1924-8, except in terms so highly abstract that you can't tell who he means. His analysis at every point relies on dealing with the State as one thing and its "apparatus" as another, as though an actual State

*Thermidor was the name given during the French Revolution to the month of July. In Thermidor 1794 the regime of Robespierre was overthrown and replaced by a bourgeois Directory.

could be abstracted from its apparatus. And so it can — as an idea. And then we are back before the revolution with nothing to explain. At the time of the Soviet Thermidor the only class remaining in Russia sufficiently reactionary and sufficiently substantial to have carried Stalin into power *against the wishes of the Party*, was the class of peasants. In fact it was the Party which carried him to power and he led it against the peasants.

Persuasion and example had met with no success. In 1928 Stalin decided to collectivize the farms by force. The ins and outs of it are tedious and awful. The thing was done, on his own estimation, at a cost of ten million peasant lives. But agricultural output didn't rise at all. There was no help for it then: industrialization also would have to be achieved by force. The mines and dams and factories would be built by forced labour.

Trotsky's passing into open opposition was a godsend to Stalin. If Lenin's closest colleague could show himself to be objectively a counter-revolutionary, who could not? The Gulag archipelago became an empire with millions of subjects. They were taken indiscriminately but particularly from the Party, and more particularly still from among the Party leadership where oppositionists might be thought to lurk. The charge of "Trotskyism" was deadly because it was vague. It was more like a witch's curse than a rational allegation. Thousands of Party Members were packed off to labour camps in utter bewilderment, searching their consciences for what they might have done. The vagueness of the charges as Kruschev says "actually eliminated the possibility of any kind of ideological fight or the making of one's views known". It was of course intended for that purpose. Most of the leadership was shot — seventy percent of the Central Committee in a single year according to Kruschev. Before execution many were brought by "barbaric tortures" to confess to "grave and improbable crimes". And so on. It is barely readable.

All this would have revolted Lenin. But it would have revolted him on unconditionally human grounds. According to the Marxist ethic as formulated by himself, there was nothing wrong with it. Whatever conduced to the building of socialism was morally acceptable. And the necessary base of socialism

13

was the State-owned heavy industry which Stalin was building. He carried out the basic programme of the Party to the hilt. And the programme had included no restrictions on the method of achieving it. Revolutionary rule was "unrestricted by any laws". All things were permitted.

Marx had said that all societies are morally autonomous, each producing a morality which reflects and justifies its practice. But whence this need to justify? Why don't societies do as they do and leave it at that? And in fact most societies have produced moralities which have not justified their practice but by which they have themselves judged their practice to be wanting. There would seem to be a continuous yearning not only for material progress but moral progress too. And Marx himself asserts that as one society has supervened upon another "there has on the whole been progress in morality". But that can only mean that there *is* a super-social and abiding morality by which progress can be judged. You cannot say one thing is better than another unless there is a standard common to them both. He frequently refers to socialism as a "higher" form than capitalism. And he stigmatizes greed and self-interest as "base and ignoble". I think that Marx was such a very moral man that he assumed an unconditional human morality even as he denied it. Whether it can be built into the Marxist system without fatally inhibiting the revolutionary impulse I do not know. But Marxists ought to be thinking about it.

They ought to be thinking too about the relationship of power and property. Is it true that the source of power is always private property so that class domination will disappear automatically with its abolition? The Bishops and Abbots of the Middle Ages did not legally own the Church estates but did in fact control them. And were in consequence conspicuously powerful members of the feudal ruling class. May not Soviet Commisars be somewhat similar? The fact that they cannot leave their power to their children may actually strengthen their class solidarity. This one's son will marry that one's daughter. There will be a sort of group inheritance. It seems to me that instead of power stemming from property, property may merely be the form of power current in our own

14

society. Marx was a man of the Nineteenth Century and property mesmerised him.

And are the Marxist laws of History really scientific laws or are they, more modestly, brilliantly creative and illuminating guesses? It is important to know. The operation of a scientific law is inevitable. The law of displacement says in effect that if a cannon-ball drops in the sea it sinks, not that it will probably sink but may decide to float; it has no choice and sinks inevitably. But for that which is inevitable no-one can be blamed. Nor, if our actions are inevitable, can we be sensibly exhorted to act otherwise. "Inevitable" is the favourite word of Marx and Lenin. Their pages are spattered with it. Yet they are spattered too with fervent praise and bitter blame and urgent exhortation. I do not blame them for failing to resolve this ancient philosophic contradiction between determinism and free will. But it is a dangerous contradiction to leave as it were lying about when what you have in mind is not a philosophical debate but bloody revolution, and when the man you are talking to may be a man like Stalin. I find no evidence to indicate that Stalin was a sadist. He was, I would say, just dreadfully thick-skinned, morally indifferent and mentally inadequate. He did what he did on the authority of men who ought to have known better. They are more to blame perhaps.

Lenin was impatient. He hurried through his life towards the revolution like a lover late for an assignation. Warnings, cautions, awkward moral questions roused his keen suspicion. Did these dubious comrades really want the revolution he was forced to ask himself, or were they at heart mere reformers, moral cowards, looking backwards like Lot's wife and pining for the ethical flesh-pots of bourgeois democracy? His was a generous impatience doubtless, but it has proved in the event to be self-defeating.

I think that the Marx-Leninist analysis of our own society is devastating and sufficient. But I think that the programme for replacing it is fatally insufficient. Marx dismissed programmes for a revolution motivated morally as utopitan and merely sentimental. In the light of events it seems that any programme for achieving utopia without such a motive is merely sentimental. The envy and resentment bred by deprivation are

15

more constant motives, being natural and automatic. But they are manifestly dangerous unless illuminated in some way.

Having said all that, let me say this too. I have mentioned that the industrialization programme was carried out in part by the employment on a massive scale of ruthlessly forced labour. Additionally let it be remembered that there were also thousands of volunteers. In that welter of injustice and the fear that it engendered, a strain of high idealism somehow survived. And Marx-Leninism continues to show itself capable of engendering this. In all those nations which are now emerging from the domination of the capitalistic West it is the chosen creed of the most dedicated and active leaders. And it attracts the generously impatient young here at home as well. It offers stimulus and hope together with a sort of massive self-certainty. In that it resembles a religion. The comparison is hackneyed but really unavoidable. Conversion to Communism is like religious conversion, all-embracing, demanding and comforting. The inconsistencies of Marxism are resolved by taking a sudden leap into commitment. In that it resembles a religion too. I wish it didn't need a leap, for that is where the trouble starts. I wish that our Marx-Leninists would address themselves to knitting up those inconsistencies, or at least would acknowledge them. But they don't.

It is hard to condemn the Bolsheviks of Lenin's generation for all their bloody-handedness. They were so much more strenuous and daring than ourselves. But then they had the advantage of not knowing the outcome. The present generation of Marx-Leninists who, having that advantage, continue to make the same assertions exactly as though the history of the last sixty years simply hadn't happened, seem to me not admirable, seem merely vehement; and idle with it. They reject any attempt or even invitation to reconsider their beliefs as the heresy of "revisionism". And this reduces Marxism from a life-enhancing method to a dead and deadly dogma.

In the course of his denunciation Kruschev told the assembled Comrades: "Stalin toyed with the absurd suspicion that Voroshilov was an English agent. (Laughter in the hall)." When Kruschev came to account for Beria who had been till Stalin's death the second man in Russia and after it the first, he described him as "the rabid enemy of our Party, an agent of a foreign intelligence service". There was no laughter in the hall at this. The charge was equally absurd but Kruschev hadn't said so. And the years of training under Stalin had taught the Comrades when to laugh. Nobody laments Beria. What is so disheartening here is the obvious device of ascribing his misdeeds to his having been an agent, in order to silence any serious enquiry into how he came to be what he actually was: another monstrous tyrant at the head of the socialist State.

I think that Lenin was an admirable man, possessed by a terribly wrong idea. It was terribly wrong because it was only partly right. And it was so absolutely punitive that it needed to be absolutely right. Of course a man must have the right idea before he can become effective, but an idea which excludes the man cannot be the right idea. Lenin would have disagreed with that, but proved it by his life and death. My play is about that.

I don't believe that those famous contradictions which threaten our society are conflicts of material interest expressing themselves as moral conflicts. I think they are moral conflicts expressing themselves as conflicts of material interest. If instead of being greedy and selfish we were compassionate and just we would not (as we do) exploit each other, and our interests wouldn't conflict. I think that socialism is, or could be, a more just arrangement than our own. But I don't believe that any arrangement will in itself get good behaviour from indifferent people.

When it first occurred to me to attempt this play I rejected the idea hastily. For one thing the Russian revolution is so fraught with urgent implications for ourselves that it is hard to see it at dramatic distance. But perhaps for that same reason the idea wouldn't go away. And then, the event was so terrible, the personalities so strenuous, the endeavour so total and the outcome so tragically far short of what they had intended that merely to think about it steadily is to be overwhelmed by primitive pity and awe. And that, so Aristotle says, is the proper stuff of drama.

Notes on some of the people in the play:

Lenin

His physical appearance is sufficiently well-known from photographs—the short, strong body, the alert head with the jutting beard and vivid, narrow eyes. It is the head of a leopard on the body of a little bull. There was something of the leopard in his character too. A merciful man could not have done some of what Lenin did or caused to be done. But he was not gratuitously cruel. Gratuitous cruelty indeed disgusted him. But so did tolerance, which he regarded as morally sluggish. He was certain of his purpose. And because he was completely given over to it he was completely integrated, which gave him a terrible energy, and completely unselfconscious, which gave him a terrible charm. He was awesome and naive. Friends and enemies alike were afraid of him but even his worst enemies never seriously debited him with a dirty motive, and his friends as Lunacharsky says were half in love with him. He was an affectionate friend when time permitted, quick to see a need and insistently attentive. But friendship went by the board when revolutionary duty called, and it constantly called. After winning an argument — and he always won by fair means or foul — Gorky describes him as habitually adopting 'a strange and rather comical stance, throwing his head back, inclining it to the shoulder, thrusting his fingers under his arm-pits, in his waistcoat. There was something delightfully funny in that posture, something of the triumphant fighting-cock, and in that moment he beamed all over, a large child in this accursed world, a splendid man who had to sacrifice himself to hostility and hatred so that love would at last be realized.' But for all his warmth, flashes of charm and abiding personal simplicity Lenin was a deeply serious man with a dangerous intention. I think we must remember first and last his overwhelming, ruthless will.

Trotsky

Handsome, brilliant, brave. 'An eagle' said Lenin after their first meeting. There were moments when their colleagues thought him Lenin's equal or superior. But only moments. Where they speak of Lenin's character, they speak of Trotsky's style. He was very aware of style—a thing of which Lenin was barely conscious. In his amazing many-sidedness, man of action, orator, scholar and thinker, he is more like a renaissance man than a man of our own times; but he had that renaissance arrogance too. He was, to be blunt, a conceited man. It breathes in all his books. And the fact that his conceit was justified by his performance didn't make it easier to take. He made enemies needlessly and, as it proved, fatally. But there is something admirable even in that; his own preoccupations were so lofty that he couldn't be bothered by the more base preoccupations of more ordinary men. He measured himself against History. He was not, except in this ultimate sense, pretentious. Rather he went in for careless elegance and wit. But his wit was stinging, and I don't know that he ever turned it on himself. However, he was not like many witty men, cold-hearted. His accounts of the revolution are full of emotion —not only his own. He really did share in the emotion of the revolutionary troops and workers he commanded and he elicited their devotion. So: a daring, somewhat daunting, charismatic man, but too swiftly articulate, not gladly suffering fools and a little condescending even in his friendship. The only person he looked up to was Lenin and that was because Trotsky too, for all his self-esteem, was dedicated to the revolutionary cause. The difference perhaps is this: One can imagine Trotsky as a brilliant success in any number of careers; one can't imagine Lenin as anything but what he was.

Stalin

Significantly, reliable *personal* accounts of Stalin simply don't exist. He had no friends before he came to power; thereafter he had only sycophants. He seems to have had no capacity for personal affection. His wife committed suicide, his son took to drink and his daughter fled. From start to finish he was alone; it is entirely possible that he was lonely. His manner of life at the end of his life was wretched and restless like that of some unhappy and dangerous animal. Alone among the Bolshevik leaders he was of plebian birth and neither widely-travelled nor well-read. He was and felt himself to be inferior in every way but one: His revolutionary dedication was primitive, well-grounded in resentment, not dependent on his understanding and so not to be shaken by argument nor inhibited by bourgeois scruples. In formulating Party policy he was slow to commit himself and when he had to commit himself early was often an embarrassment. Yet Lenin thought so highly of him that at the time of Lenin's death Stalin (again alone among the leadership) had a seat on every important organ of power. Lenin took for granted the high purpose of the Party and mistrusted too much talk about it. The respect which he felt for Stalin was the respect which he felt for the down-trodden masses, who had learned their revolutionary function not from Marx but from their own intolerable treatment by society as it stood. A proletarian who thought a little was a more reliable revolutionary than an intellectual who thought a lot. Stalin would do what needed doing. After Lenin's death Stalin did what needed doing to collectivize the land and industrialize Russia, thus completing the basic (that is economic) Marxist programme, the declared programme of the Party. In doing it he turned the Party and the State machine into a sort of bloody treadmill with himself as the plodding horse. Whether Lenin would have done the same or left the programme incomplete is the unanswerable question which one can't help asking. And whether Lenin came to understand that motives of resentment, however natural, are negative, and can't be satisfied by any positive achievement, I do not know and rather doubt. What is certain is that Lenin came to understand that Stalin was no mere wheel-horse at the service of the Party but an envious, sly and implacable enemy of anyone and anything which stood between himself and the ultimate reassurance of ultimate power. But he came to understand this only when it was too late. And Stalin proved to be as brutal and malevolent against his revolutionary peers as he had been against the erstwhile ruling class. Nobody survived his rancour. To achieve prominence and popularity was to be marked down for death. But this came later. At the period covered by the play he is a limited, slow-burning, solitary man, not more than half aware of his own malignant appetite, not machiavellian but instinctively cunning, carefully filing each affront, hoarding his hatred. Trotsky describes his glance as 'yellow-eyed' and hostile. His expression in the photographs is shut. Except for his blue-black hair and Caucasian moustaches he was neither physically nor facially striking. But like Peter the Great this man took Russia by the scruff of its neck and tore it from one epoch to another. His death, as described by his daughter, has a sulphurous operatic grandeur, a touch of Ivan the Terrible. He can't at any time have been merely a clown; he must have had a dangerous dormant strength as well as dangerous limitations. I think this part needs to be cast and played with that in mind.

Gorky

In appearance and character everyone's ideal Russian. He was tall and strongly built, but early privations had inflicted the disease which at length killed him. His face was primitive and powerful, with a broad forehead and high cheek-bones, but rendered complex by the melancholy eyes. His writing is not (as was later claimed) proletarian but picaresque. He had immense compassion for the suffering of the poor but what he chiefly dwelt on was the unpredictable eccentricity, passive or violent, which such suffering engenders. He was not, though Lenin thought him so, a sentimentalist. He had no illusions, as Lenin had, about the regenerative powers of popular vengeance. Peasant vengeance in particular he feared. He loved and respected Lenin but he was not afraid of him. And Lenin, though he violently resented Gorky's violent criticisms of the Bolshevik regime, never threatened Gorky nor would permit him to be threatened. Gorky was a long-time champion of the Revolution, its 'stormy petrel'; he had put his purse and reputation at its service. Also, they were friends. They quarrelled, when they did, as equals. And for all that Lenin scoffed at Gorky's agitated indignation, he coveted his good opinion. Gorky had a knowledge of life at the lower depths which Lenin never came near; he had risen from those depths with an inner moral dignity which commanded the respect of such disparate and perceptive persons as Tchechkov and Tolstoy. He was fascinated by humanity, knowing it at its worst, longing for it to be better, but concerned for it as it was, not as it might become. So: humour, quick appreciation, moral strength held in reserve, courtesy and—perhaps most

21

important—a certain detachment. After all he was, finally, an artist not a politician.

Lunacharsky

John Reed in his book *Ten Days that Shook the World* describes him in October as flashing-eyed and student-like. Contemporary photographs show a man in early middle-age, untidily dressed, with a big sedentary body and a mild, kind, thoughtful face, a bit like a good doctor. He had no gift for violence but was, after Lenin and Trotsky, the most popular of the October leaders. He thought the Revolution a new dawn and he communicated his high expectations with a candour and enthusiasm which endeared him to his armed and starving audiences, whose experience of life had not been so uplifting. Lenin never talked about the New Jerusalem, Lunacharsky never stopped. He it was who burst into tears and resigned from the Council of Commissars when it was learned in Petrograd that in the course of the coup in Moscow, the beautiful domes of the Kremlin had been shelled. Lenin persuaded him to resume his post when it was later learned that only two shells had struck, one of which had failed to detonate and the other done minor damage to a part of the palace of small architectural interest. He was intimate with the avant garde among the poets, painters and musicians of revolutionary Petrograd and was often to be seen in their company, walking rapidly, talking excitedly, overcoat flapping. As Commissar for Education and Enlightenment he made himself their patron. But he had a deep respect for traditional culture and opposed the iconoclasm of those who demanded 'a Cultural October'. The educational policies of the Commissariat under his regime were both humane and practical but came to nothing, mainly from the desperate poverty of Russia at that time, but partly from his own ineptitude. Stalin's educational policy was ruthlessly utilitarian and Lunacharsky ended his days as a sort of roving ambassador in Europe, which he loved. His defence of Stalin's Russia was sad and half-hearted but unwavering; he was, he insisted, a Bolshevik before anything else. What he particularly and predictably admired in Lenin was his strength of will. Lenin regarded Lunacharsky with alternate pleasure and exasperation.

here was nobody, according to Krupskaya, whose company
enin more enjoyed, but in serious matters he found him 'soft'
–a severely approbious term.

Dzerzhinsky

He turned from his aristocratic background to the revolution as
a youth. He was constantly in prison. At once fastidious and
romantic, he was the kind of man who gets caught. He was too
sensitive and too high-minded for his own or anybody's good.
He had lyric expectations of the socialist revolution, which he
confided to his diary, and only these, he said, restrained him
from despair and suicide. He is a man then who suffers but,
being a gentleman, keeps his suffering to himself. Inwardly
gentle and diffident, his outward manner will be severe—one
of those men whose controlled and frosty features dissolve into
a smile of touching innocence, and take you by surprise. He
took an active part in the October coup and was appointed to be
Commandant of the Bolshevik and Soviet Headquarters in the
Smolny Institute. He performed this modest function in an
exemplary way, treating all arrivals, important or obscure with
the same quiet, courteous suspicion. It was not until he was
appointed to the Cheka that he became a figure of fear.
Precisely because he hated the work he did it without pity,
conscientiously. I imagine a sharp change in his outward manner
here; he is trying to reduce himself to the status of a thing, a
weapon. Even his colleagues became a bit afraid of him and at
the time of his death he was pathetically and rather awfully
concerned to assure himself of their affection. As the apparatus
of the Cheka grew he was increasingly absorbed in keeping it
clean and efficient. At no time did he use the power which was
accumulating in his hands for any but its proper purpose—the
enforcement of the Party's will. Because of that the Cheka came
to be regarded as inviolable and unquestionable. And because
of that it could of course be used for any purpose. His death
was much lamented. With good reason. He was succeeded
first by Yagoda and then Yezhov, a swift descent from the
puritanical to the perverse. The only picture I have seen of this
Perfect Knight of the Revolution' shows a strong, round,

hairless head, the face severe but calm, the eyes untroubled behind rimless spectacles.

Krupskaya

In her youth she was, I would say, very nearly beautiful, with strong but feminine features, a slightly scornful mouth and marvellous truthful eyes. Her expression is not aggressive but quite fearless; one understands that this would not be a person lightly to cross on a matter of principle. Later she thickened, and was inclined to be dowdy. As a girl she wrote to the great Tolstoy a letter which is worth quoting (condensing) because it reveals the fundamental sweetness and steady fervour of the later woman: 'Esteemed Lev Nikolaevich! . . . Recently I have felt more and more keenly that up to the present I have benefitted by the labour of others . . . When I read your letter to the young ladies of Tiflis I was so glad! I know that the work of correcting books which the people will read is serious, that great ability and knowledge is needed for this, and at eighteen I still know too little . . . But I appeal to you with this request because, perhaps, through my love for the work I shall succeed somehow in helping my lack of ability and ignorance . . . Pardon me for having disturbed you with this request, I took you from your work . . . But surely it will not occupy you for specially much time. N. Krupskaya.' Her devotion to Lenin was absolute but not uncritical. On their first meeting he mocked her 'Good Works' among the proletariat and she noted 'something evil and arid in his laugh' and she insisted in recording that impression in her famous *Memoirs of Lenin* after his death. When they arrived in Russia together in 1917 and Lenin shattered the Bolsheviks with his demand for immediate, red revolution Krupskaya turned to a nearby Comrade and mildly observed, 'It appears that Vladya is out of his mind.' In the years preceding, in their wandering exile, not only had she uncomplainingly cared for her leonine husband but had acted in effect as Secretary to the mainly conspiratorial Party using amateur codes and invisible ink. (This ink was made visible by the application of a flame and their apartment was full of the smell of burning paper). But after the Revolution she was relegated to comparatively unimportant work in the

Commissariat for Education and held no important post except, willy-nilly, the post of First Lady. Most likely Lenin thought it would smack of nepotism for his wife to hold high office in the Party or the State. Like him, she remained personally modest, even in her case a bit diffident. After his death she became a sort of mother-figure to the Russian masses, receiving daily scores of pleas for help and intervention. Stalin brought every kind of pressure to bear upon her but she never became, as did most of the others, Stalin's creature. She was forced to re-edit her *Memoirs* with the assistance of a Chekist secretary but she refused to exaggerate Stalin's part in the revolution or to put into Lenin's mouth Stalin's abuse of Trotsky. She had that fastidious, lady-like strength of character which one sometimes still encounters in surviving sufragettes. She retained to the end not only her courage but her humour. Books, particularly children's books about her late great husband were commonly submitted to her approval. On one such occasion 'If this is another one saying that Uncle Vladimir wants them to clean their teeth and do their homework, I won't read it' she said. One last anecdote to illustrate their relationship. When in 1914 the socialists of the Allied and the Central Powers signified their support for the Imperialist War, Lenin was at first incredulous and then disgusted and enraged. He was reading an equivocating statement made by the German Socialist leadership. 'These people are shit!' he exclaimed. From the open kitchen door came a mild, reproving 'Vladya!' Lenin hesitated, looked towards the kitchen and repeated 'Shit!' On a note of defiance.

Kollontai

She was a novelist, a poet and free-thinker. In particular she believed in free-love. In theory all the early Bolsheviks eschewed marriage as a bourgeois device for turning women into property and all believed in free-love. But Kollontai, unlike Krupskaya in this instance, practised what she preached. 'There are only two real Communists in Russia', said the Menshevik leader Martov 'Lenin and Kollontai'. (When Lenin heard of this he laughed and then, wistfully, 'What a clever man Martov is' he said. They had been close colleagues and friends in the early days and now were political enemies.) When Trotsky announced to the Workers, Soldiers and Peasants of the Soviet, the success of the October coup, Kollontai stood with tears streaming down her face as the desperate audience rose and rendered first *The Marseillaise* and then *The Internationale*. She wept again when, as Commissar for Social Assistance she had to use troops to take over the Tsarist Ministry building and funds. But she was highly and joyously intelligent as well as highly emotional, and her view of her colleagues, even of Lenin, remained drily and dauntlessly personal. She was popular with everybody. She became a leader of the short-lived Democratic Opposition to Stalin's dominance of the Party and after Lenin's death Stalin found diplomatic duties for her, outside Russia.

CAST OF FIRST LONDON PRODUCTION

State of Revolution was first presented by the National Theatre Company at the Lyttleton Theatre, London, on 18 May 1977. The company was as follows:

In order of speaking—

Lunacharsky, Anatole Vassilyevich	
	Stephen Moore
Dzerzhinsky, Felix Edmundovich	
	John Normington
Lenin, Vladimir Ilyich	Michael Bryant
Gorky, Alexey Maximovich	Brian Blessed
Kollontai, Alexandra Mihailovna	
	Sara Kestelman
Minister	Trevor Martin
Stalin	Terence Rigby
Martov	Anthony Douse
Spiridonovna	Catherine Harding
An Anarchist	Michael Stroud
Russian General	Godfrey James
Chelnik, a sailor	John Labanowski
Old Soldier	Louis Haslar
Officials	Antony Higginson
	John Pollendine
Soviet Soldier	James Leith
Krupskaya, Nadezhda	June Watson
Captain Draganov	Michael Stroud
Policeman	Peter Tilbury
Trotsky, Leon Davidovich	Michael Kitchen
Von Kuhlmann	Peter Gordon
General Hoffman	Edwin Brown
Count Czernin	Anthony Douse
Fany Kaplan	Sarah Simmons
Advani	Godfrey James
Pratkov	James Leith
Dr Geutier	Anthony Douse

with Roger Gartland, Julia Pascal, Diana Payan, Andrew Tourell, Drew Wood

Director	Christopher Morahan
Designer	Ralph Koltai
Lighting	David Hersey
Assistant Lighting Designer	Brian Ridley
Staff Director	Harry Lomax
Assistant to the Director	Laszek Burzynski
Production Manager	Martin McCallum
Stage Manager	Jackie Harvey
Deputy Stage Manager	Ernest Hall
Assistant Stage Managers	Catherine Bird
	Paul Greaves
Sound	Jim Douglas
Assistants to the Designer	Tony Jones
(Costume)	Gaelle Allen

ACT ONE

A lectern standing in a single spot. The rest of the stage is dark.
Lunacharsky enters. Applause on speakers. He smiles in
acknowledgement and:

Lunacharsky: Thank you . . . Thank you . . .

> *He gets quiet.*

Thank you. It is always a pleasure to address the Young
Communists. To see . . .

> *He peers benevolently across the lights.*

Yes, I can just see—the faces of the future as it were. Open,
smiling, ready for anything. And you know, these anniversaries of Comrade Lenin's death are not for those of us who
knew him altogether sad occasions. Rather are they happy-sad.
I make no apology for the personal note. The personal of
course is marginal. The historically determined movement of
the masses is alone decisive. As you know from your studies of
Karl Marx and as our great revolutionary leader J. D. Stalin is—

> *Instantaneous and prolonged applause on speakers. He*
> *waits, then joins in and when at last it stops.*

—is always at such pains to emphasize. But Comrade Stalin
would himself agree I think that on these occasions a personal
note is unavoidable and even in its way illuminating. So then.
I will introduce you to Vladimir Ilyich some years before the
revolution, in the home of Alexey Maximovich Gorky, on the
island of Capri. Capri, as some of you may know is a play-

ground of the international bourgeoisie in its more light-hearted, less obviously offensive aspects. But you may be sure than V. I. Lenin was not there to play. Nor for the matter of that was I. We were getting ready there a school for advanced Party activists. I had prepared a paper for this school. And on the very day when Vladya came to us from Switzerland, I was submitting it to the approval of the other lecturers. Including Comrade Lenin. I remember to my shame that as I came to my conclusion, I felt rather pleased with it—

> *Lights up. Outdoors, a hot day. Capri 1910. Seated on the ground or on cane chairs,* **Dzerzhinsky**, **Gorky**, **Kollontai**, *all in light summer clothes, and* **Lenin** *in the waistcoat and trousers of a dark tweed suit.*

—because this conclusion is a dialectical conclusion. It does not challenge the reality of matter, but allows its interpenetration by what may loosely be termed spirit. It does not challenge our revolutionary ethic, but allows its interpenetration by the best of the christian liberal ethic, the ethic if you will of love. Thus synthesising for the first time in our History an unconditionally human ethic. And in my submission this is perfectly compatible with both the tone and teaching of Karl Marx.

> *He finishes, timedly excited.*

That's it.

> *A pause.* **Dzerzhinsky** *to* **Gorky**.

Dzerzhinsky: It's brilliant.

Lenin: It's what?

Gorky: Brilliant.

Lenin: I'm glad that Capri has been good for your lungs Alexey Maximovich. Your mind seems to have collapsed. His thesis is shit.

Kollontai: A really excellent thesis Anatole Vassilyevich. *(to* **Gorky***)* I think we should open the school with that.

> **Lenin** *rounds on her, dangerous.*

Lenin: Now—

Kollontai: —Don't bully me Vladya, I won't have it. If you have objections to the thesis, please let us have an orderly discussion.

Dzerzhinsky: And let us if we can confine ourselves to decent language.

> Lenin *considers him. He looks back at* Lenin *fastidious and unflinching.* Lenin *controls himself.*

Lenin: I withdraw the word 'shit'. Substitute 'excrement'.

Kollontai: You consider that appropriate?

Lenin: Highly appropriate—it's a nicer word for the same nasty substance. And Lunacharsky's thesis is Marxist in its terminology and in its substance, unashamed idealism!

> *An overlapping chorus of protest:*

Dzerzhinsky: Not at all, not at all—

Kollontai: It was nothing of the kind.

Gorky: You haven't listened, Vladya.

Kollontai: He's completely missed the point, Tolly.

Lenin: Look, have you all gone mad?

Kollontai: It seems improbable, why do you ask?

Lunacharsky: Look, may I speak?

Kollontai: Yes, go on 'Tolly. *(She repeats)* He's completely missed the point.

> **Lunacharsky,** *to* Lenin, *placating.*

Lunacharsky: There is a negated idealism in the dialectic, natur—

Lenin: — Your silly sing-song had as much to do with dialectic as the Holy Roman liturgy.

> **Kollontai** *exasperated.* **Gorky** *smiling but reproving:*

Gorky: Oh come on Vladya. This is not discussion, this is mere abuse.

Lenin: It merits abuse. Why do you want to discuss it?

Dzerzhinsky: 'Why'?

Lenin: Yes. Why?

Dzerzhinsky: Because we are not your creatures Comrade Lenin. But revolutionary Comrades. With opinions of our own.

Kollontai: And happen to be the majority.

Lenin: Oh—!—Oh I *see* . . . the *majority*. It's not a school for revolutionary activists you're getting ready here—it's a school in Parliamentary procedure. Well I would say that you are very well equipped.

Dzerzhinsky: This is intolerable.

Lenin: Intolerable?

Dzerzhinsky: Yes!

Lenin: That's the first revolutionary utterance I've heard from you all day.

Dzerzhinsky: My revolutionary record—and that of everybody here is at least as honourable as your own.

Lenin: True—

> *Rising, lugging a note from his pocket.*

Here are—ten lira. Towards a glass case for your records. You can run a revolutionary museum too!

> *He is going. But—.*

Lunacharsky: Vladya—

> **Lenin** *stops. Turns, goes to him. Soberly:*

Lenin: We need a school for activists because we are living through a period of dreadful inactivity . . . Is that not so?

Lunacharsky: Well yes, of course—

Lenin: In such a period the only thing that can see us through is unconditional class hatred. And unconditional human love is nothing but a dirty dream. Why are you still in the Party?

> **Lunacharsky** *appalled, the others shocked.*

Lunacharsky: What?—

Gorky *(uncomfortable):* Vladya—

Kollontai: How dare you, Vladya—Shame.

Lenin *(ignores them):* Well? Why?

Gorky *(sharply):* Stop it Vladya.

Lenin: What's the matter 'Tolly? Can't you tell me? Don't you know?

Lunacharsky: Vladya, please—

Lenin: What?

Lunacharsky: I am very much distressed—!—You know how greaty I admire you.

> *He can't go on.* **Lenin** *deliberately:*

Lenin: I have no use for your admiration. I spit in your distress.

> *He goes, upstage.*

Lunacharsky: Excuse me.

> *He goes, stage left.* **Kollontai** *follows.* **Gorky** *gloomy,* **Dzerzhinsky** *coldly disapproving.* **Gorky** *shrugs, at which* **Dzerzhinsky** *moves, picks up a book and:*

Dzerzhinsky: Of all the vices gratuitous cruelty is the least sympathetic.

Gorky: He doesn't think it is gratuitous; he thinks it's necessary.

Dzerzhinsky: Mm. Necessary to his purposes or necessary to his nature?

Gorky: He isn't cruel by nature.

He shakes his head, but he is looking at his feet, thinking his own thoughts.

Dzerzhinsky: How else?

Gorky goes, sits heavily at the chess table.

Dzerzhinsky: From what I've seen today, Alexey, Trotsky is the greater man, both personally and politically.

Gorky: Mm. Well I shouldn't say so.

Dzerzhinsky: I shall certainly say so.

Kollontai comes back wearing a shawl and carrying a lamp. They look at her.

Gorky: Where's 'Tolly?

Kollontai: He's in the music room. He's horribly upset.

She turns up the lamp. Light changes to night. Piano music from stage left. She sits. Puts on her spectacles and picks up a book.

Kollontai: If Vladya is not careful he will find himself quite isolated.

Gorky: Hey-ho . . .

Dzerzhinsky closes his book with a snap.

Dzerzhinsky: Finish the game?

He sits with Gorky at the game. They concentrate.

Now let me see . . . Ah yes.

They concentrate. Piano music off, 'Fur Elise'. Lenin enters upstage on tip-toe, as not wishing to disturb the music. Kollontai sees him and coldly:

Kollontai: Good evening Vladya.

They look up. Lenin smiles, nods, puts his fingers to his lips and tip-toes to a seat by Kollontai, elaborately friendly and humbly considerate. He listens a little. Then leaning towards her:

Lenin: Anatole Vassilyevich?

Kollontai: Yes.

Lenin: What a marvellously accomplished man he is.

Kollontai: You upset him horribly this afternoon.

Lenin: What—? Pooh—He's not a weakling.

He clasps his hands behind his head and tells them, complacently and a shade reproving:

You are all inclined to underestimate Anatole Vassilyevich.

Dzerzhinsky stares from Lenin to Gorky and back. Lenin smiles at him, goes to the table, stoops and peruses the game seriously.

Lenin: Is he good?

For answer Gorky gives a rueful grunt and indicates some vulnerable situation on the board. Lenin makes a sympathetic sound.

Mm. Your move?

Gorky: Yes.

The music stops. Gorky prepares to move a piece. Lenin sucks in his breath and:

Lenin: Tt-t-t-t.

Gorky: What?

Lenin: The bishop.

Gorky looks again.

Gorky: Oh yes.

He moves the bishop. They look at Dzerzhinsky who moves a piece and impassively:

Dzerzhinsky: Garde.

Lenin and Gorky scrutinize the new situation then Gorky looks up at Lenin and drily:

Gorky: Thank you.

Lenin: Wait a bit, wait a bit . . .

He peers a moment at the board then straightens up and airily:

Yes, well, I would never have got myself in that position in the first place.

Gorky laughs, Lunacharsky enters. He eyes Lenin warily, but:

Lenin: Bravo, bravo. Music like that it's almost better than living, you're a dangerous man 'Tolly.

Lunacharsky: I see.

He goes and gets his papers.

Life is discordant and I have chosen harmonious death.

He takes them and sits.

Well allow me to observe that if I did not think that life could be harmonious—and beautiful—yes and spiritual—I would not be, as I am, a revolutionary.

Lenin: No, nor would I.

Kollontai: Oh Vladya, no more.

Lenin: All right . . . There's an amazing steam yacht in the harbour, flying the Russian flag.

Gorky: Belongs to Feodor Lipkin; he comes here every year.

Lenin: Sensible fellow. *(To* **Lunacharsky***)* Have you seen it?

Lunacharsky: Yes, it is, beautiful.

Lenin: Mm. Are Lipkin's cotton-mills beautiful too?

Lunacharsky: Lipkin's mills are circles of Hell.

Lenin: Then what shall we do with his yacht? Because it is by any standards beautiful; it's very nearly spiritual; I dare say there's a piano on it. And a library of books and paintings; and thin-skinned ladies who can play the piano, and sincere broad-minded gentlemen who know what's in the books and understand the paintings. It's a vessel of culture is Lipkin's yacht. But because of Lipkin's mills, it must go down.

He sits close to his victim, gentle and serious.

Now that's the contradiction. And no thesis can resolve it because it is an actual contradiction which only action can resolve.

Lunacharsky: Well of course it is! But—

Dzerzhinsky: Nobody here is afraid of action.

Lenin *looks at him with interest, then back at* **Lunacharsky**.

Lenin: But?

Lunacharsky: It is a very *painful* contradiction!

Lenin: And?

Lunacharsky: And I suggest that you remember that.

Lenin: And Anatole Vassilyevich, my dear, kind-hearted Comrade, I suggest that you forget it.

Lunacharsky: You never in your life 'suggested' anything.

Lenin: Well I like that—!—

Kollontai: It's perfectly true. Talking to you is like standing in front of a firing squad.

Lenin: . . . What a stupid image . . .

35

I'm pleased to meet you Felix Edmundovich.

Dzerzhinsky *inclines stiffly. Makes no other response.*

Lenin: Where did you learn to play chess?

Dzerzhinsky: I learned in prison. *(Adds very distinctly)* In Nineteen Five.

Lenin: Ah . . . You had a good teacher.

Dzerzhinsky: Brilliant.

Lenin: He's a brilliant man.

Dzerzhinsky: A magnificent man.

Lenin: Yes he is a bit that way inclined.

Dzerzhinsky: In Nineteen Five he was magnificently right.

Lenin: I said so at the time.

Dzerzhinsky: You haven't said so recently.

Lenin: He hasn't been right recently. Or do you think he has?

Dzerzhinsky: I think he has deserved more generosity than you have shown him recently.

Lenin: Mm. Yes I see how Trotsky might attract you. Magnificence and generosity. You ought to be on Lipkin's yacht. They've got all the moral amenities there.

Kollontai: And must they go down too?

Lenin: I don't know, perhaps they float.

Lunacharsky: But Vladya, Vladya—What if they don't?

Lenin looks at him, goes to him, serious and winning.

Lenin: I don't know what, I can't anticipate. Each new society gives birth to virtues of its own. Not even you can dream them up. My friend, there is no peace, no comfort for the human spirit yet. It is fighting to be born.

Lunacharsky: That's very fine.

Lenin: It is?

Lunacharsky: Oh yes. It's terrible, but it's very fine.

Lenin: Well there we are then.

He takes the papers from him and tears them across, smiling cheerfully.

Lunacharsky: No! *(Steadily)* No Vladya.

He takes them back. **Lenin** *doesn't resist, but quietly:*

Lenin: If you are going to disseminate this enervating rubbish among active Party workers, I will have you expelled from the Party.

Kollontai: Try it!

Lenin: Are you?

Lunacharsky: I don't agree with your assessment, Vladya. And—

Lenin: —Alexey Maximovich, I'm going home tomorrow. Can you arrange it?

Gorky: Tomorrow—! Yes I can arrange it . . .

Kollontai *(stiffly):* Goodnight Vladya.

Lunacharsky: Vladya . . .

No response. **Kollontai** *sweeps out, he follows.*

Dzerzhinsky: Good-night Comrade Lenin.

He accompanies it with a stiff little bow. **Lenin** *turns his head to watch him out.*

Gorky: What do you make of him?

Lenin: All right . . . Bit pure.

Gorky: Are you really going to expel 'Tolly?

Lenin: If I can.

Gorky: You used to be very fond of him.

Lenin: Still am very fond of him. What's that got to do with it?

Gorky: I think it ought to have something to do with it.

Lenin: Well. For a writer of fiction, a suitable thought.

Gorky: Good-night.

Lenin: It's ages since we met. Let's talk.

Gorky *turns, wary of the sudden change of tone.*

Lenin: How is your health?

Gorky: I've told you.

Lenin: Mm. Mother Nature isn't markedly maternal is she?

Gorky: Off and on.

He straddles a chair.

Lenin: Mm.

Gorky: Vladya, are you fond of Stalin too?

Lenin: Stalin?

Gorky: Yes.

Lenin: The Caucasian?

Gorky *is looking down now.*

Gorky: Yes.

Lenin: I hardly know him. I like what I hear.

Gorky: What do you hear?

Lenin: That he does what needs doing, and doesn't make a hobby of his soul. *(And as* **Gorky** *looks up)* Oh you don't

37

make a hobby of it—you make money at it.

Gorky: Are you going to ask for money?

Lenin: We're desperately short, Alexey.

Gorky: What happened to the money from the Tiflis bank raid?

Lenin: I know nothing about the Tiflis bank raid.

Gorky: Don't you—?—I do. Kamo did it, on Stalin's instructions. Stalin instructed him, at your instigation. And you got the money.

A beat of stillness. Then:

Lenin: Who told you?

Gorky: Never mind who told me Vladya; I want an explanation. It was ruled at Party Congress that there were to be no more of these disgusting robberies.

Lenin: Expropriations.

Gorky: —Robberies—!—You have made us look like a gang of thieves.

Lenin: In bourgeois terminology we are a gang of thieves.

Gorky: We heard all that at Congress, I don't want it again. An explanation, Vladya, or I shall ask for it in print.

Lenin *considers this. Then:*

Lenin: In the bourgeois Press?

Gorky: Would you let me use the Party Press?

Lenin *cornered.*

Lenin: Well. The Party had no money and the Party needed money. In order to survive you know. It's quite important to the Party that the Party should survive.

Gorky: We heard all that at Congress too.

Lenin: And having heard what did you do?

Gorky: By an overwhelming vote we decided what should not be done!

Lenin: In the perfect confidence that I would do it.

Gorky: Vladya, have you really such contempt for everybody but yourself?

Lenin: In the perfect confidence that somebody would do it. Well?

Gorky: I'm thinking. *(He nods and admits)* Perhaps. I'm not sure. But yes, perhaps.

Lenin: You're an honest man.

Gorky *looks at him but doesn't answer.*

The money from the raid is all in big notes, numbered; we can't use it. Are you going to give me some or not?

    Gorky *takes a packet from his pocket.* **Lenin** *counts the contents.*

Lenin: Oh . . . Thank you.

Gorky: You frighten me.

Lenin: Not really.

Gorky: Oh yes, really. I know what you think is wrong with the world; but what world do you want?

    Lenin *sits and glowers and grumbles and then:*

Lenin: All right I suppose you've paid for it. I want a world where men like you will not have to torment themselves. And men like me . . . You really love this kind of conversation don't you?

Gorky: Go on.

Lenin: Men like me will not be needed. Now you've had your money's worth. Let's go in.

Gorky: And men like Stalin?

    Lenin *checks, dangerous.*

Lenin: I don't know about men like Stalin. But if he's needed he'll be there. If we had more men like him and fewer men like you my friend, the revolution would succeed.

Gorky: Perhaps. But Vladya, what would it succeed in doing?

Lenin: Don't let's quarrel, let's go in.

Gorky *(shrugs):* All right.

    He gets up, gloomily. Begins to gather up the chess men. **Lenin** *watches him. He wants to patch it up.*

Lenin: You know you'd save yourself some torment now, if you'd read a little Marx.

Gorky: Oh yes?

Lenin: Big events aren't formed by people, people are formed by big events.

Gorky: Mm.

    Lenin *casts about for something more to mollify him with.*

Lenin: I couldn't expel Anatole Vassilyevich, even if I wanted to.

Gorky: No?

Lenin: No. Too popular.

Gorky: Good.

He begins to relax. **Lenin** *becomes mischievous. Approaches, tip-toe, glancing back at house, and, gossipy:*

Lenin: Would I, er—would I have to expel Alexandria Mihailovna too?

Gorky *(smiles):* Yes.

Lenin: I thought she was with whatsisname—the Austrian?

Gorky: Oh Lord no, that was six months ago.

Lenin: My word she doesn't change.

Gorky: No.

Lenin: Free love and vegetables.

Gorky *(protesting):* Oh—

Lenin: Oh there's more to her than that. Course there is. Fine Comrade. So's he really. Oh yes, they'll be all right when things burn up again.

Gorky: Are things going to?

Lenin: Burn up? Yes I think they are. I think there's going to be a war, Alexey. A big one.

He makes it sound promising.

Gorky: And would you welcome that?

Lenin: What? Good heavens—can't you get it through your head? If there's going to be a war, Alexey, it won't wait for my welcome!

They go. Blackout and the roar of guns. White spot on the lectern. **Lunacharsky** *enters. Waits until the guns have faded. Then:*

Lunacharsky: It was a war which turned the world into a stockyard. With the workers of the world for stock. We Russians lost six hundred thousand men within the first six months: two million when the records cease, and after that uncounted numbers . . .

He hesitates, then:

Comrades, we have recently encountered, among broad sections of the peasant masses, a wrong-headed resistance to the vital project of collective farming. We are overcoming this resistance by patient education. And, where needs be, by revolutionary direct action. And some of you I fear have been led by this necessity to adopt a hostile and superior attitude towards the peasants as a whole. Comrades, that is very wrong. It was the peasant armies of the Tsar who made the revolution. And those of you who are assigned to the collectivization stock brigades would do well to remember that. Be patient, Comrades. Be—consistent with your revolutionary duty—merciful . . .

He has said as much as he dare.

Remember that of all the armies then engaged, it was the Russian peasant who at length refused that shameful service. And this so suddenly that all of us were taken by surprise. Except for Comrade Lenin. His arrival at the Finland Station is of course a twice-told tale. Though I for one can never weary of it. But what you have to understand are the extraordinary contradictions in the situation he confronted. The Tsar had gone, we had a democratic constitution. We had indeed the most completely democratic constitution which the world had ever seen. The entire programme of the bourgeois revolution was accomplished in the month of February. To proceed immediately to the proletarian revolution seemed historically impossible. Should we then support the February Government? How could proletarians support the bourgeoisie? The Kaiser's Army meanwhile was rolling over Russia. And the Kaiser was the champion of the international reaction. Yet could we ask the Russian masses to go back to the slaughter of their Comrades in the German Army? And yet again how could we not? I—

Lights up on **Minister** *and two* **Officials** *at a table.* **Party Politicians** *seated in a row. Crowd of desperate looking* **Soldiers** *and* **Sailors,** *including* **Zhelnik,** *a gigantic sailor, is held back by guards.*

—for my part Mr Minister will gladly leave these questions in firmer hands than mine.

Minister: Thank you, Mr, er—

Consulting papers. But **Stalin** *rises, goes to lectern, and:*

Stalin: J. D. Stalin for the Bolshevik Party.

Martov *(standing):* Object. The Bolsheviks are not a Party.

Stalin: For the Bolshevik faction of the Social Democratic Party.

41

Martov: Thank you. *(Sits)*

Stalin: The Bolshevik faction being as it is the faction of the proletariat—

Martov: Object. My faction has an equal claim to be the faction of the proletariat.

Minister: On come along, Mr Martov, after all it's only rhetoric.

Stalin: And being as it is the faction of the peasants—

Spiridnovna *(rising):* Object!

Minister: Oh look now. *(Throws down his pencil)* Ladies and gentlemen—

Anarchist: Object.

Minister: Ladies and Gentlemen, Comrades, Citizens, Brothers and Friends. I know that listening to other people is an unfamiliar inconvenience, but well, you see, that is democracy. Now Mr Stalin has the floor. It's a madhouse.

Stalin: Being such a faction the Bolsheviks do not address themselves to the February Government, which is the Government of capital, wage-slavery and brutal exploitation.

   Official *looks up indignantly and opens his mouth.*

Minister: Oh let it go, for Heaven's sake.

Stalin: Nor do we address ourselves to the Menshevik faction, which is the faction of compromise and class-betrayal.

Martov: Object. I'm sorry Mr Minister, object in the strongest possible terms.

Minister: Over-ruled.

Stalin: Nor do we address ourselves to the so-called Social Revolutionaries, who are the Party of adventurism and revolutionary fraudulence.

   Spiridnovna *leaps up.*

Minister: No! Look—the principle is simple. You will all have an equal opportunity to call each other names—but you cannot do it all at once. Mr Stalin.

Stalin: Nor do we address ourselves to the Anarchist Party, which is the Party of lunatics, hooligans and gangsters.

Anarchist: Object! Order!

Minister: The Anarchist wants order—

Stalin: And least of all do we address ourselves to the Party of Kadets . . . which is the party of reaction.

Minister: Object?

General: Not in the slightest.

Stalin's wooden manner drops. Baleful:

Stalin: The Party of insolent arrogant privilege; the Party of the Past.

General: That remains to be seen my friend.

Stalin: Yes. For which reason Comrades we address ourselves directly to the armed and revolutionary proletariat and peasants!

Applause. **Soldiers** *and* **Sailors** *bang their rifle-butts on floor.*

Our programme is the expropriation, total and uncompensated, of the capitalist and landlord classes!

Applause as before.

We are uncompromisingly, unwaveringly and intransigently hostile to the capitalist and landlord classes!

Applause as before.

We are uncompromisingly, unwaveringly and intransigently hostile to imperialistic war!

Applause as before.

However—

Puzzled silence.

The war is no longer imperialistic. The Kaiser of the Germans is the cousin of the Tsar. And if his armies conquer Russia he will return it to the Tsar. It is therefore our revolutionary duty to resist his army. This is obvious. This is inescapable. Comrades, this is the historic task.

Minister: And, er, this is your programme?

Stalin: It is our immediate programme.

Minister: Well it seems very sensible. Mr Martov?

Martov: My faction reluctantly supports this programme.

Minister: Splendid. Maria Spir—

Spiridnovna: The programme of my Party is the programme of the people! The land to the Peasants—!—expropriate the great estates!

Applause as before. **Minister** *with exasperated patience:*

Minister: Maria Spiridnovna I have said repeatedly: that if the Constitutional Assembly should decide upon expropriation, expropriation will ensue! And since it is to be elected on a universal franchise, it will presumably express the wishes of

43

the people.

Zhelnik *fires his rifle into the air.*

Minister: You have a question?

Zhelnik: Yes. How much longer do we wait for this Constitutional Assembly?

Minister: Oh, well, that I cannot say—

Zhelnik: Thought as much. Comrades it's a trick.

Minister: My dear good chap, how could I say? Imagine what's entailed in counting forty million votes.

Soldier: It'd take an educated man a good long time would that.

Zhelnik: Comrade, you're a fool.

Soldier: You mind your mouth.

Zhelnik: I tell you it's a trick!

Minister: It is not a trick!

> **Zhelnik** *fires his rifle again.* **Minister** *resigned announces:*

The Assembly will convene no later than November.

Spiridnovna: Then the Social Revolutionaries too reluctantly support this programme.

Minister: And the Anarchists?

Anarchist: Abstain.

Minister: General?

> *The* **General** *is silent for a moment, then:*

General: Well, if you're going to expropriate my estate you're going to have to fight for it. There may be one or two bits missing— *(He flaps his empty sleeve)* But I'm still man enough for that. I'll fight for what is mine. And that includes my country.

Martov: Well, that includes nine thousand acres of it anyway.

General: Yes. More than my fair share no doubt. But I had it from my father and I'll fight to leave it to my son. As any one of you that's man enough to have a son would fight for what is yours. And Russia is your country too.

Spiridnovna: —Don't listen Comrades!

General: What? Oh Madam, these brave fellows aren't your comrades; they are mine. We've been through a good deal together. Isn't it so lads?

Soldier: I was with you at Tannenburg, Sir.

General: Were you—?—Good for you. Now in November I'll be voting for His Majesty the Tsar. Because I think that power is proper to a gentleman and poison to a politician. But if you'd rather take your orders from committees of commercial travellers and money-lending yids—all right, your privilege. You've earned it, you've fought for it. But any man who'll see his country overrun by Prussians, Krauts, and pansy, dancing, Viennese is a yellow-bellied bastard!

He rides down the uproar.

And that's what's happening! Tell them Minister!

Minister: Men, the German Third and Seventh Armies are advancing unopposed!

Official: Committing unheard-of and bestial atrocities!

2nd Official: The Front is open!

On speakers, anthem, cheering and church bells, into which the General roars:

General: Well lads—what about it?

The din is interrupted by the blast of a locomotive whistle. They freeze.

The light begins to darken. Lenin enters in travelling clothes and carrying a bunch of red flowers. Krupskaya follows with a gladstone bag.

Minister: The Provisional Government of National Unity welcomes the return of V. I. Lenin.

Lenin: Am I not to be arrested?

Minister: Good Heavens no, those days are over.

Lenin: That's bad, that's very bad. Who here is from the Soviet?

Soldier: The Petrograd Soviet of Worker Soldier Deputies welcomes your return.

Lenin: Where are you going, Comrade?

Soldier: Well, to the Front.

Lenin: Has the Soviet ordered you to the Front?

Soldier: Well, not to say the Soviet . . .

Lenin: Then—

He steps forward, rips the red band from Soldier's sleeve. A stir and murmur.

Stalin: This is the line of the Party. This is the line of the Central Committee.

Lenin: It is?

Stalin: Adopted nem con, by the Central Committee.

Lenin: Merde, to the Central Committee.

Lunacharsky: Vladya, it was only after very long and serious debate that we—

Lenin (*clearly and distinctly*): Shut up.

> *He looks at the red band in his hand, thrusts it at* **Soldier.**

You have no right to this.

> *He turns on his heel, goes to the lectern, the others flinching away from him. The light has darkened dramatically now,* **Lenin** *casting a giant shadow, the others lit fitfully. He becomes the* **Lenin** *of the famous photographs. He hammers home his arguments like nails into a plank, staccato.*

Lenin: Comrades, what is the purpose of this war? You do not know. And they who made it do not know. Yet those who made this war are dying in it just as you are. And are powerless to stop it. Has it then no purpose? It has no conscious purpose. But it has inexorable causes. It is the last obscene convulsion of a dying system, of a morally exhausted ruling class. The war will stop when the People take power. Unless they take power the war will continue. In Russia the People have taken power and the war has already stopped.

Official: Tell that to the Germans!

Lenin: The German people know it. The Russian Revolution will become World Revolution, if the Russian People do not falter. But the Russian People are afraid.

> *The giant* **Zhelnik** *wanders towards him, fascinated.*

Afraid of a word. That word is 'Government'. All Government is finally based on force. All force is finally armed force. The armed forces of Russia have declared allegiance to the Soviets. Therefore the Soviets are the Government of Russia. And when the Soviets declare allegiance to the Provisional Government they declare allegiance to an empty word.

Minister: This is treason!

Lenin: I call for treason.

Anarchist: This is anarchy!

Lenin: It is the very opposite. I demand for the Soviets absolute authority. I demand for the People the means of production. The land to the Peasants, the places of work to the urban workers. Now! I call upon the front-line troops to fraternize with their German comrades. Now! I call upon the garrisons to turn their rifles on their Officers. Now! The programme is immediate and bloody civil war! And if that means a German victory—I call for Russian defeat!

His speech has had the effect of a boot on an ant-hill. **Lenin** *stands stock still, a pariah. Everyone exits. Light change to warm interior.* **Krupskaya** *takes his coat and goes. He thrusts his hands into his pockets and whistles softly 'Fur Elise'. She returns without her hat and coat but with a vase; glances at him and begins to put the red flowers in it. He stops whistling.*

Lenin: Well? What do you think?

Krupskaya: I think you are out of your mind.

Lenin: Oh.

Krupskaya: Also, I think you are uncertain.

Lenin: Oh? Why do you think that?

Krupskaya: When you are certain you don't ask what I think.

Lenin: Hm. Nadya don't desert me, now.

Krupskaya: Oh, you *are* uncertain . . .

Lenin: Support me.

Krupskaya: Support you in Committee?

Lenin: Yes.

Krupskaya: How can I Vladya? That speech was crazy. We are in a classically defensive situation and you are calling for the barricades! No-one will support you.

Lenin: No-one?

Krupskaya: Who—? Dzerzhinsky—No. Lunacharsky—?—No.

Lenin: —No. Lunacharsky doesn't *want* the barricades. He wants to addresss the Duma! In a frock-coat—!—with a white carnation in his button-hole!

Krupskaya: Always you defend yourself by attacking someone else. He is a loyal Comrade; and utterly sincere.

Lenin: Well perhaps it'll be a red carnation . . . Zinoviev might agree with me.

Krupskaya: Not this time; much as his likes agreeing with you.

Lenin: What about Kollontai?

Krupskaya: She of course will agree with her lover.

Lenin: Yes? Who's that?

Krupskaya: How should I know? I haven't seen her for six months.

Lenin: Nadya, you're a prude.

She looks hurt. He goes to her hastily.

So am I, so am I . . . *(He kisses her forehead)* Support me . . .!

Krupskaya: I *can't*, Vladya . . .!

She looks at him distressed as he leaves her and stands apart, back turned.

Lenin: Stalin?

Krupskaya *(a beat, then short):* Yes, perhaps.

Lenin: You don't like Stalin, do you?

Krupskaya: Do you?

Lenin: If I had to rely on the people I like, I'd go back home tomorrow.

Krupskaya: Does that include me?

Lenin: Apparently.

He sits with her at the table.

Krupskaya: You are stupid about Stalin, Vladya.

Lenin: No. You are stupid about Stalin. You chose to be a revolutionary from the goodness of your bourgeois heart. A man like Stalin is a revolutionary from the circumstances of his birth. And for that there is no substitute.

Knocking at the door, off. They look at one another. Knocking again.

Krupskaya: Go on.

Both go. He to hide, she to the door. It is routine. Voices. **Kollontai** *enters, rapidly.*

Kollontai: Vladya—?

Lenin *comes back.*

Oh Vladya, Vladya, what a speech—!—What a—Oh! *(She embraces him)*

Lenin: You agree with me?

Kollontai: Does anyone disagree?

Krupskaya *enters.*

Lenin: Oh yes.

Krupskaya *looks at* **Lenin** *drily, looks off.*

Krupskaya: Come in, Comrade.

The giant sailor **Zhelnik** *enters, still carrying his rifle.*
Kollontai *goes to him, brings him to* **Lenin.** *Shyly:*

Kollontai: Vladya, this is Comrade Zhelnik.

Lenin: Ah. *(Shaking hands)*

Kollontai: He is a sailor.

Lenin: Yes. Does he agree too?

Zhelnik: That speech was a bull's eye.

Kollontai: A bull's eye. The arrow to its mark. Yes. He wants to join the Party.

Krupskaya like Lenin has been suppressing a smile, but now:

Krupskaya: To join? Alexandraya are you mad? This is a terrible breach of security—!—How long have you known this Comrade?

Kollontai: Oh, I think he can be trusted Nadezhda.

Krupskaya: You 'think'—?

Kollontai: He is a member of the Kronstadt Sailors' Soviet.

Lenin: Oh. Is he?

Kollontai: His shipmates elected him.

Lenin: Do your shipmates agree with my programme too?

Zhelnik: We can't shoot our officers.

Lenin: Why?

Zhelnik: We drowned the Captain. And the rest have gone.

Lenin: Oh.

Kollontai: The Captain was an awful creature—awful!

Lenin: What kind of ship is it?

Zhelnik: Heavy cruiser. The 'Aurora'.

Lenin: You have expropriated a heavy cruiser?

Zhelnik: Right.

Lenin: Can you go through with it?

Zhelnik: Got no option, now.

Lenin: Oh see how clearly they see it—! Have you got guns?

Zhelnik: Six inch and eight inch.

Lenin: No—rifles.

Zhelnik: They're in the armoury . . . Armoury's locked.

Lenin: But, can't you break in?

Zhelnik: We've broken nothing yet. Ship's as smart as she ever was. Admiral's inspection if you like.

49

Lenin: Strict, revolutionary discipline.

Zhelnik: Strict. Right.

Lenin: Oh what a Comrade. Still, break into the Armoury.

Zhelnik: Right.

Knocking again. **Lenin** *curses softly and, going, says to* **Zhelnik:**

Lenin: Stay.

Krupskaya *too has gone as before.*

Kollontai: You've made a good impression on him.

Zhelnik: That's nice. He's made a good impression on me. You can tell him if you like.

Kollontai: Fedor Gavrilovich—don't be so *proud* . . .

They look at one another. This unlikely couple is in love. Voices off. **Stalin** *enters.*

Kollontai: Yosef.

Stalin *(grunts):* What's he doing here?

Kollontai: Vladya wants him.

Stalin *grunts again.* **Krupskaya** *comes back, her arm linked in* **Gorky's,** *followed by* **Lunacharsky** *and* **Dzerzhinsky** *who go off after* **Stalin.** **Gorky** *coughing.*

Krupskaya: Are you all right?

Gorky: Yes, yes.

He sits. All sit. Silence. **Lenin** *enters with papers. Looks at* **Gorky,** *doesn't speak. Sits and concentrates on papers. Silence uneasy.*

Gorky: Vladya—

Lenin: Just a minute. Are you a member of the Central Committee?

Gorky: No. But if you carry the Committee, I am going to leave the Party. I thought the Committee would like to know.

A stir.

Kollontai: Alexey, you can't.

Lenin: If I don't carry the Committee, I may leave the Party.

Consternation.

Krupskaya: Vladya, you're possessed.

Lenin: Yes!

Krupskaya: A month ago you said that revolution was not to be looked for!

Lenin: A month ago we were in Switzerland! I didn't look for it

—I found it!

Gorky: Where did you find it?

Lenin: On the streets—!—*(Roaring)*—Where would you expect to find it?

> *He glares round, twitching with suppressed anxiety. Forces himself back to his papers, hunched and dangerous.*

Gorky: You are possessed by vanity and crude excitement. What you have found is nothing better than desperation.

Lenin: What better could there be?

Lunacharsky: Vladya, couldn't we talk about this, calmly?

Lenin *(bitterly):* That I dare say we could manage.

> **Lunacharsky** *looks round.* **Krupskaya** *nods encouragement, urging him on.*

Lunacharsky: What revolution are we talking about, Vladya?

Lenin: Oh go to b— . . . Wait.

> *He rubs his hand hard down his face, fighting for control.*

I beg your pardon.

> *His face is white, his voice unnaturally flat.*

I am talking about social revolution.

Gorky: And what you will get is a peasant rising! Mindless, bloody and barbaric. Reaction may come of it. Chaos may come of it. But socialism cannot.

Lenin: Why?

Krupskaya *(despairingly):* Because that can only come from proletarian revolution, Vladya!

Lunacharsky: And we have no proletariat! We have no proletariat to speak of. Surely, this is elementary . . .?

Lenin: It is a simplified abstraction. I am looking at what I can see. You are remembering what you have read. I see no peasants on the street. I see soldiers and sailors.

Gorky: They are peasants all the same. And when the peasant talks of revolution, he is thinking of a meadow. And when he understands the difference between socialism and a meadow he will hate your revolution from the bottom of his soul.

Lenin: No.

Gorky: Goddammit—I was born a peasant!

Lenin: But now, you're a middle-class literateur.

He goes to **Zhelnik.**

He was born a peasant too. But now he's a conscripted sailor. And a man in uniform who mutinies is revolution incarnated. And all that's needed is for us to articulate *his* demands!

Gorky: What are your demands, Brother?

Zhelnik: Stop the war. Take the land.

Lenin: Correct.

Gorky: But who will the land belong to then?

Zhelnik: Us.

Lenin: Correct.

Gorky: To you—Individually? Or everyone collectively?

        Zhelnik *looks at him, narrowly.*

Lunacharsky: What Comrade Gorky means is—

Zhelnik: —I know what he means. (*To* **Gorky**) Big question.

Gorky *(laughs):* Ho—ho. What's the answer?

Zhelnik: We'll cross that bridge when we come to it.

Lenin *(quietly):* Correct. By God correct. I do not say the revolution is certain of success. I say we have the means to attempt it. Here. *(His hands on* **Zhelnik's** *shoulders)* And now. The choice is therefore either to attempt it now. Or admit that we don't want it. And never really did.

Lunacharsky: That's not a choice that's moral blackmail.

Lenin: If it feels like blackmail you're feeling guilty. Yosef, what do you think?

Stalin: I am waiting for the other Comrades.

Lenin: Clearly. While you're waiting what do you think?

Stalin: I think your line is theoretically correct. However, I doubt if it is practical.

Lenin: If it isn't both it's neither. You're talking like a fool.

Krupskaya: He's talking sense.

Lenin: Why is my line not practical?

Stalin: In my opinion to organize the masses we need time to build a massive Party. This—

Lenin: If we take the line the masses want, we will be massive overnight! Felix Edmundovich—what do you think?

Dzerzhinsky: I think your line is Trotsky's line. What do you think about that?

Lenin: I think so little about that, that if you will not follow me, I will follow Trotsky.

Consternation. Exclamations.

Kollontai: Vladya, I agree with every word you've said. But you cannot split the Party—now.

Lenin: There are rotten elements inside the Party that the Party can't afford just now. *(He is looking at* **Gorky.** *Knocking off)*

Let them in as you go out. *(He turns away as* **Gorky** *goes)*

Krupskaya *(to* **Zhelnik***):* You must go now too, Comrade.

Lenin: He can wait a minute.

Noise off. A burst of voices and a slamming door. **Gorky** *comes flying back.*

Gorky: Police!

Lunacharsky: What—?

Gorky: Police!

All but **Krupskaya** *rush off stage. A uniformed* **Policeman** *rushes on, and off after them. With him, walking,* **Draganov,** *an anonymous official. He holds out his hand to* **Krupskaya** *and says politely:*

Draganov: Papers?

She gets them from her bag and gives them to him. **Policeman** *comes back.*

Policeman: I think they've given us the slip, sir!

Dragonov: Oh. Well do what you can.

Policeman *rushes off again, fumbling for his whistle. We hear it, off, receding.* **Draganov** *returns the papers.*

Thank you.

Krupskaya: May I go?

Draganov: Yes.

Krupskaya: I thought the Secret Police had been disbanded, Captain Draganov.

Draganov: Ah. Yes. But it's not the kind of thing you can do over-night you see. At your service . . . At anybody's service actually. A technician you know, just a technician.

Policeman *rushes on, breathless:*

Policeman: They have—!—They've given us the slip!

Draganov: Oh dear, what a pity.

Policeman: You don't seem very concerned!

Draganov: Oh I am—Oh yes—After them!

Policeman *rushes off again.*

Draganov: An enthusiast. These are difficult times for a man like that. A certain flexibility seems indicated. One doesn't know which way the cat is going to jump.

Krupskaya looks at him, wary and non-commital.

Does one?

Krupskaya: No.

She goes. He muses:

Draganov: And such a cat.

The lights go out with an electric hiss. He looks up.

That for instance. Is it I ask myself a show of revolutionary strength by the comrades at the generating station? Or an authorized power-cut? Is God at home or not?

He strikes a match, burns his fingers.

Shit. It's important to know. And daily more difficult.

Lights up on a different scene. **Minister** *enters.*

Minister: The vital thing is a sense of proportion. One must not see catastrophe where perhaps there is no more than a healthy show of popular initiative.

Draganov: No, Minister.

Minister: On the other hand, Draganov we cannot assume that the times in which we live are not catastrophic, merely because it is we who live in them. After all, someone has to live in catastrophic times.

Draganov: Yes, Minister.

Minister: Mm. You're an intelligent chap Draganov, how would you describe the situation?

Draganov: . . . Fluid.

Minister: You don't just rush to commit yourself, do you Captain?

Draganov: I am as you say an intelligent chap.

Minister looks at him with little liking for a moment.

Minister: Mm. I tried to get a table at the 'Belle Etoile' last night . . . couldn't. The most expensive restaurant in Petrograd—bursting at the seams. You can't get in to 'Gudonov', you can't get in to Karsavina. And Faberge declares that he has never done such trade. Does that look like revolution?

Draganov: Er . . .

Minister: You're absolutely right, it does. The workers at the

Putilov have occupied the factory, and the Seminovsky guards decline to move them out. The Bolsheviks have occupied the Smolny Institute. And nobody would even dream of trying to move them out. Nobody indeed would dream of going near the place. In my opinion Draganov these people at the 'Belle Etoile' are spitting in the wind. Where do they obtain their pâté and cigars? I will tell you. They obtain them at the frontier with the assistance of the frontier guard. The patriotic officers deploy the secret funds with which you have so lavishly provided them in night clubs. In my opinion, Draganov, the Russian upper, middle, middle-upper and blue-blooded classes merit overwhelmingly whatever happens to them.

Draganov: It's, er . . .

Minister: Yes?

Draganov: It's a little late in the day Minister, but I'm beginning to respect you.

Minister: Thank you Draganov. I have always entertained for you the liveliest feelings of loathing and contempt. Ah, General–
> **General** *enters.*

—You know our good Draganov.

General: Yes.

Minister: Captain?

Draganov: The practical plans for insurrection have been put in charge of the man Bronstein—Trotsky. Ulyanov—Lenin is still in hiding but I'm pretty sure he's here. The date of insurrection depends upon the Minister. The signal will be gunfire from the battleship 'Aurora'.

Minister: In what sense does the date depend upon myself?

Draganov: The date for the Constituent Assembly will be the date of insurrection—or perhaps a couple of days before.
> *The* **Minister** *nods, looks away, and, to no-one:*

Minister: . . . Why?

Draganov: They are determined at all costs to anticipate the Assembly.

Minister: But why? This man Ulyanov—This latest document of his— *(He picks up a pamphlet)* 'State and Revolution' . . . It does not seem unsympathetic? It is if anything dottily idealistic. He seemingly expects the Brotherhood of Man

55

within a generation. Why then will he not allow the people to declare themselves?

Draganov: He is quite certain that they will.

Minister: It's a very strong position . . . Well, General?

General: The Second Don and Kuban Cossacks are ready to move at twelve hours' notice. With artillery.

Minister: I have told you repeatedly: I will not use Cossacks!

General shrugs. **Minister** *quietly:*

Will you or will you not accept the High Command?

General: I cannot deal with Bolshevism if my officers must deal with Bolshevik Committees. And if I cannot shoot deserters I cannot keep an army in the line against the Germans.

Minister: To dissolve the Committees is politically impossible. And I regard the shooting of deserters as an atavistic horror.

General *(contemptuous):* Your day is done sir.

He goes. Light fades. Mob noise distant.

Minister: Oh what a pity, Draganov . . . What a pity.

A cannon shot. Everyone freezes. The distant howl of the approaching shell grows louder and louder, becomes inescapable. At the moment of impact BLACKOUT and SILENCE. A telephone rings. Stops. LIGHTS UP. The stage is red. The telephone stands on the table. **Trotsky** *has the receiver to his ear. He is watched by* **Stalin, Dzerzhinsky, Kollontai, Krupskaya, Lunacharsky.** *All have rifles.* **Lenin** *is seated, his face in his hands, exhausted.*

Trotsky: Very well . . . Good. *(He puts down the receiver. Says to* **Lenin***:*

It's done.

Lenin *takes his face from his hands, rubs it.*

Lenin: Tell them.

Trotsky *advances on the audience.*

Trotsky: Comrades! Last night Red Guard Detachments together with detachments from revolutionary Kronstadt, took command of Petrograd. *(Applause on speakers)* The central telephone exchange, banks, bridges, post and telegraph bureaux, police stations and railway termini are ours. Warrants have been issued for the arrest of the bourgeois Government and the Winter Palace is surrounded.

(Applause) Comrades, they will say that we are men of violence; they will say that we are adventurers. I, Leon Davidovich Trotsky, reply in your name—yes—we are embarked upon that violent adventure which goes by the name of Human History! Comrades they will say we have created chaos, that we have turned society upside down. I reply—no—we have turned society right way up. It is right that the people should take command—and right that you should obey! *(Applause)* Comrades, the left wing liberals and right wing socialists, the moderates, the Mensheviks, will demand a part in our Government. I reply to these Gentlemen—no—it is a revolutionary Government and you took no part in the revolution. Away with you—to the dustbin of History! *(Applause)* Our Party, Comrades, is not a machine for gathering votes—It is the weapon of the working-class! Comrades, here is the swordsmith who hammered that weapon: Vladimir, Ilyich—

> *As* Lenin *steps forward the rest of it is lost in applause from speakers: tumultous, hoarse, punctuated by individual ecstatic cries. He stands unmoved as it billows about him: at last holds up his hand; it ceases.*

Lenin: We will now proceed to the construction of the socialist order. The People's Commissar for Welfare.

Kollontai: Effective from today, all ranks, degrees and titles are abolished. All who work are free and equal!

Lenin: For Nationalities.

Stalin: All Peoples of the Russian Empire being free and equal peoples have the right to self-determination!

Lenin: For Security.

Dzerzhinsky: The Office of Magistrate is abolished. Police interrogation is abolished. Trial and investigation are the office of the open People's Courts!

Lenin: For Foreign Affairs.

Trotsky: The People's Commisariat proposes to the Allied and the Central Powers an immediate, democratic and honourable Peace, without loss or detriment to any Nation!

Lenin: For Education.

Lunacharsky: All children of the Russian People have an equal right to an enlightened education!

Distant fire of heavy guns. All but **Lunacharsky** *hear it and react, but he, absorbed:*

All children, Comrades, will therefore enter similar schools at an equal age. First, the kindergarten school. These kindergartens, Comrades, will not be institutions for the manufacture of skilled labour, no, they will be pockets of the future, full of morning light—

Zhelnik *enters and goes to* **Trotsky**; *the others gather and listen, gravely. But:*

—from where all children equally will have the right to scale the highest pinnacles of culture. Comrades, to this end—

Lenin *and the others leave.* **Zhelnik** *comes to* **Lunacharsky**.

Zhelnik: Comrade—

Lunacharsky *nods, smiles, but holds up his hand and continues:*

Lunacharsky: —To this end, Comrades, the People's Commisariat decrees throughout all Russia, polytechnical, coeducational and self-administrating schools!

Zhelnik: Comrade—

Lunacharsky: What—?

He is impatient of the interruption, but looking round he sees the empty stage and registers the booming guns.

Oh. What—?

Zhelnik: The Cossacks, Comrade. Are you coming?

Lunacharsky *is torn between his revolutionary duty and his cultural enthusiasm.*

Lunacharsky: Yes. Yes of course. Each school council will comprise teachers, senior pupils and representatives of the local working population!

Rattle of machine-gun, close.

Teachers to be subject to election!

Zhelnik: Comrade!

Lunacharsky *waves him to be silent, breathless, wanting to get it all in before he goes.*

Lunacharsky: In each school week, one and one half days will be for club activities and out of door excursions! All schools will provide free hot breakfasts!

Small arms fire, closer. **Zhelnik** *goes.* **Lunacharsky** *goes after him, drops his papers, retrieves his papers, drops his rifle. Sorting himself out:*

Homework, punishments and compulsory examinations are abolished!

He goes. Cannon booms. The light grows cold. Machine-gun fire prolonged and vicious. Three banners are lowered, the Imperial eagles of Germany and Austria, the red flag of the revolution. With them, a chandelier. **Trotsky** *enters, left, with briefcase. Takes papers from it. Then clasps his hands behind his back and muses upwards at the chandelier.* **Kuhlmann**, **Czernin** *and* **Hoffman** *enter, also with briefcases.*

Kuhlmann: Good morning! Good morning! *(Glances at his watch)* What admirable promptitude. Er, von Kuhlmann.

Extends his hand. **Trotsky** *hesitates, takes it, wipes his hand on the seat of his trousers. Unperturbed* **Kuhlmann** *rattles on.*

For Austria, Count Czernin. And General Hoffmann for the High Command.

Trotsky: Gentlemen.

They sit, business with papers while:

Kuhlmann: I should like some coffee. Coffee gentlemen? Coffee Mr Trotsky?

Trotsky: Thank you no.

Kuhlmann: Well perhaps not; I drink too much coffee, far too much. *(Sitting)* Are your quarters satisfactory? Please don't hesitate, if there is anything that you would like . . .

Trotsky: I would like to get on.

Kuhlmann: Admirable. *(Consulting his papers)* And the terms of your proposal are admirable too. Germany for the Germans, Russia for the Russians—Austria of course for the Austrians; and no hard feelings. Admirable. But I feel you should address these terms to the aggressor nations, France and Britain.

Trotsky: We have done so.

Kuhlmann: May I know with what result?

Trotsky: With no result.

Kuhlmann: Well there it is you see. I fear that Germany and

59

Austria can only stop the war, by winning.

Trotsky: Or by losing.

Kuhlmann: Or as you say by losing. Here on the Russian Front however—I don't know how to put it with sufficient delicacy —but here we do seem to have won—would't you say?

Trotsky: You have stolen a great deal of our territory, Herr von Kuhlmann, yes.

Kuhlmann: I do so much admire the steadily moral nature of Mr Trotsky's preoccupations. But you see Mr Trotsky it isn't just that we have taken some of your territory. We are in a position to take a lot more. *(To* **Hoffmann***)* I think that is so?

Hoffmann: We could be in Petrograd by April.

Trotsky: No.

Hoffmann: Without the slightest difficulty.

Trotsky: No.

        Hoffmann *puts his booted feet on the table and:*

Hoffmann: Your defences are deserted; your armies are in rags.

Trotsky: The armies of Bonaparte fought in rags.

Kuhlmann: You have a Bonaparte?

Trotsky: We have a revolution. If you advance on Petrograd, our ragged armies will defend it to the last drop of their blood.

Kuhlmann: Oh Mr Trotsky come along; rags and blood are the weapons of rhetoric.

Trotsky: I don't deny that German Generals—almost it would seem by nature—have very superior boots.

        Kuhlmann *smiles,* **Hoffmann** *scowls and takes his feet down.*

But there is still one excellent army between you and Petrograd.

Kuhlmann: Oh?

Trotsky: Your own.

Kuhlmann: You think our soldiers would refuse to march?

Trotsky: You would be ill-advised to let them march to Petrograd.

Kuhlmann: Why, what would they see there that is so appealing?

Trotsky: Their comrades, in command.

Czernin: *Your* comrades, in command.

Kuhlmann: And that you see is less appealing; the German people Mr Trotsky do not like your Revolution.

Trotsky: Then how do you explain the January Soviet which appeared in Berlin?

Kuhlmann: Ough. A handful of traitors, it died in a day.

Trotsky: It was bloodily put down, by troops.

Kuhlmann: Yes, the troops were most indignant. Their morale is very high just now.

Czernin: And how do you explain the demonstrations which appeared in Petrograd when you dismissed the Constituent Assembly?—Were they not bloodily put down by troops?

Trotsky: Yes, the troops were most indignant. They were demonstrations by the bourgeoisie.

Czernin: According to your writer Gorky—whose work I very much admire—they were demonstrations by the workers. And he is most indignant.

Trotsky: I too admire his writing.

Hoffmann: Is this a military conference or a philosophical debate?

Trotsky: The two are not distinct. Believe me Herr von Kuhlmann, your morale is merely military; ours is Revolutionary. Bring your troops to Petrograd and you bring dry straw to a naked flame.

Hoffman: Not straw Trotsky; steel.

Kuhlmann: In matters of philosophy the General, like you, believes in a material reality.

Trotsky: Flame is a reality.

Kuhlmann: But steel is the material in question. Now the terms you have proposed are—

Trotsky: —Admirable.

Kuhlmann: Please—? Ah—*(An appreciative little laugh)* Admirable, yes. But not acceptable.

Trotsky: No?

It has a note of appeal, but:

Kuhlmann: No.

Trotsky: Then what would be sufficiently contemptible?

Kuhlmann *(apologetic):* Reality.

Trotsky: We couldn't just this once, attempt to make reality admirable?

61

Kuhlmann: Oh that I must leave to you Mr Trotsky, I really don't feel up to it.

Hoffmann: You take our terms. Or fight.

Trotsky *(to* **Kuhlmann***):* According to your terms you take two-thirds of our coal and iron, one third of our factories, a million miles of territory and sixty millions of our people.

Kuhlmann: Approximately.

Trotsky: How can we take such terms?

Hoffmann: I don't think you can fight.

Trotsky: Count Czernin, I am dealing here with Prussian Policemen, you embody in your own esteem six centuries of Christian culture. If you take the Ukraine, this winter we shall starve. Is that what you desire?

Czernin: The question is unfairly phrased. There is no question of our 'taking the Ukraine'. The People's Government of the Ukraine has signed a separate peace.

Trotsky: And thereby showed that it was not a People's Government.

Czernin: The People voted for it.

Trotsky: That means nothing.

Czernin: Oh . . .! *(To* **Kuhlmann***)* Do *you* understand?

Kuhlmann: I think so, yes. If the Ukrainians had a People's Government in Mr Trotsky's definition, they would have the right to self-determination, provided that they did not exercise it, and the right to vote, for Mr Trotsky. It's really very similar to any other Government.

Trotsky: Very. All Government is similar, and similarly vile. Our aim is to dispense with it. Meanwhile, you use troops to shoot down men, we use troops to shoot down masters; the only difference being that a different man gets shot; which hardly matters.

Czernin: Well. Candid anyway.

Trotsky: Yes that's another difference. When we take power we take responsibility; we know that we must do vile things. You do vile things and use the democratic to spread responsibility so thin that no-one feels responsible. And that is why while you are drifting from disaster to disaster, we shall drive on to success.

Kuhlmann: Time is on your side in fact?

Trotsky: Oh yes indeed.

Kuhlmann: Then clearly we must cut time short. One week Mr Trotsky. Then we march.

> *They get up and go.*
> *Light changes to the grey of Moscow as* **Lenin, Stalin, Lunacharsky, Kollontai** *and* **Dzerzhinsky** *enter and sit.*

Lenin: Well?

Trotsky: We take their terms or fight.

Dzerzhinsky: We fight then.

Lenin: What with?

Dzerzhinsky: Bare-handed if we must. (**Lenin** *impatient*) —I'm serious, Vladya. It would be better in the long run for the Revolution to go down with honour, than survive on terms like these.

Lenin: The honour of the Revolution consists in surviving. On any terms it can.

Dzerzhinsky: We must defend it then.

Kollontai: We must fraternize too.

Dzerzhinsky: And fraternize of course.

Lenin: I see. Shoot with one hand and wave with the other?

Lunacharsky: But—Vladya, I find this most extraordinary. The rank and file of the German Army is the German proletariat.

Lenin: And?

Lunacharsky: They will know that we are not defending Russia, or even Russia's Revolution, but the German Revolution too.

Lenin: Anatole Vassilyevich. If you're in a trench and someone's shooting at you from another trench it must be difficult to understand that his intentions are progressive. And I doubt if we could get an army to go back into the trenches anyway. (*To* **Trotsky**) Could we?

Trotsky: I doubt it. Why do you ask me?

Lenin: If you can't do it, I don't see which of us can.

> **Stalin** *glowers and shifts in his seat.*

Trotsky: I couldn't do it in a week.

Stalin (*growls*): Well of course you couldn't.

Lenin: Then in view of the fact that we have no army I suggest that we don't fight. And in view of the fact that these are the terms I suggest that we accept them.

Dzerzhinsky: Never.

63

Kollontai: No.

Lunacharsky: We *can't* accept these terms, we *can't!*

Trotsky: If we accept these terms I think the country may reject the terms and us, together.

Lenin: The country will do no such thing; you are thinking—all of you are thinking—of your own good names! I am going to put it to the vote again; and if you vote like that again I will offer you my resignation.

Dzerzhinsky: I will accept your resignation before I will accept these terms.

Lenin: In favour?

Lunacharsky: —Wait—. Vladya, I think they will take the Ukraine.

Lenin: Well of course they will take the Ukraine—!

Lunacharsky: Have you thought what that will mean?

Lenin: Yes, I have thought what that will mean. In favour?

Stalin: Yes.

Lunacharsky *(whispers):* Yes . . . Good God . . .

Kollontai: Yes.

Dzerzhinsky: No.

Lenin: Comrade Trotsky?

Trotsky: . . . Abstain.

Lenin: Carried.

   Signs the document.

Lunacharsky: Good God . . .

Lenin: How long *would* it take to raise an army?

Trotsky: We could raise a voluntary army in a month.

Lenin: Would it be any good?

Trotsky: It would be very good but very small.

Lenin: How small?

Trotsky: Too small.

Lenin: Conscription?

Trotsky: Yes.

Kollontai: What?

Trotsky: And death for desertion.

Lunacharsky: *What?—*

Lenin: Be quiet Anatole; you know nothing about it. *(To Trotsky)* Suppose that you could raise an army—Could you lead it in the field?

Trotsky: . . . Yes.

Lenin: Sure?

Trotsky: Yes.

Stalin: We seem to have found our Bonaparte.

Trotsky: That remark is very nearly, though not quite, as stupid as it is insulting.

Lenin: Er, Comrade Stalin meant no insult Leon—

Trotsky: Then he exhibits an alarming ignorance not only of the counter-revolutionary role which History bestowed on Bonaparte, but also of the Marxist view of History. I wonder Comrades if we ought not to club together for the purchase of some not too difficult Marxist primer for the use of Comrade Stalin?

Lenin: Leon, enough.

Trotsky: Very well, enough.

Lenin: Thank you. Now I propose—

Trotsky: —There cannot be a personal dictatorship without a dictatorial society. The 'Man of the Moment' is not a 'great man', he is merely the man that the moment needs. And it is not my fault if the revolutionary moment of October did not appear to be in any very urgent need of Comrade Stalin.

Lenin: Enough! You both did your revolutionary duty in October; as you both invariably do. Now let us have no more of this. Please.

Stalin: Storm in a teacup.

Lenin: Good. Now I propose that Comrade Trotsky should give up his present duties and take on the Commissariat for War.

Trotsky: No. In view of the comparison which has just been made it is an honour which I can't accept.

Lenin: You will accept; try not to think of the honour. Oh. *(Passing the treaty document)* Your final diplomatic duty. Put your name on that.

> But **Trotsky** *looks down at the document thoughtfully and doesn't move.* **Lenin** *watching him:*

Your name does seem to mean a lot to you.

> **Stalin** *gives a short laugh and signs the document* **Lenin** *takes it:*

Lenin: Thank you Comrade.

Stalin: Oh I haven't got a name.

He puts his boots up on the table. **Lenin** *waves the document to dry the ink.*

Lenin: An historic document Leon Davidovich, you've missed an opportunity.

He looks at **Dzerzhinsky**. *The document stops waving.*

Dzerzhinsky: I still regard this document as absolutely fatal. If you want me to resign I will.

Lenin: In what way is it fatal?

Dzerzhinsky: It is fatal to our honour. And our honour is essential.

Lenin: I don't want you to resign. I want you to accept the most important task of all.

Dzerzhinsky: Oh?

Lenin: . . . The Cheka.

The others go still. **Stalin** *softly takes his feet down.* **Lunacharsky** *incredulous.*

Lunacharsky: *Felix?*

Lenin: Yes.

Dzerzhinsky *(calmly, almost amused):* I couldn't do it.

Lenin: Why?

Dzerzhinsky: Vladya, I have spent three quarters of my adult life in prisons . . . You understand? I'm not talking about exile—I'm talking about prisons, I'm talking about prison cells, I'm talking about torture. The very presence of a policeman makes me physically sick! Now I know it must be done and I thank you for your confidence. But you might as well ask me to clean the streets by eating garbage?

Lenin: Do you think it should be done by someone with an appetite for garbage?

Dzerzhinsky: You are perfectly merciless . . . You should do it.

Lenin: I haven't the time.

Dzerzhinsky *(to* **Lunacharsky***):* What shall I do?

Lunacharsky: I'm horribly afraid that Vladya is right, Felix.

Stalin: We're talking about a lot of liberals. It doesn't matter who does what. What matters is what's done.

Lenin: Correct. May I put it to the vote?

Dzerzhinsky: Very well.

Lenin: In favour—?

They show.

Carried.

Dzerzhinsky gets up and goes. They look after him.
Then **Lenin** *on a note of finality, cheerfully routine:*

Thank you, Comrades.

They gather up their papers and go. **Lunacharsky**
lingering says something, sadly, shaking his head.

Lunacharsky: Poor Felix . . .

Lenin: What?

Lunacharsky: Poor Felix.

Lenin: Oh go away.

Lunacharsky going, turns:

Lunacharsky: I—

Lenin: Go away!

Lunacharsky goes.

Stalin: You're fond of him all the same.

Lenin: Yes I am. And you had better be fond of him Josef.
He's the future.

Stalin: Bit soft for me.

Lenin: Well, I wouldn't want you in charge of children.

Stalin: You don't seem to want me in charge of anything,
much.

Lenin: Are you very keen to be in charge of something?

Stalin: I'd like to be useful.

Lenin: You are without exception the most useful Comrade on
the whole Committee.

THE CURTAIN FALLS

ACT TWO

Lunacharsky *alone on stage.*

Lunacharsky: The common canteen in the Party Headquarters was operated round the clock. It was continuously crowded and· the din was always deafening. One day when I was eating there a perfect silence fell. And looking up I saw an elderly woman, oddly dressed, very tall and very thin, and with her five emaciated wolfhounds. 'Give me some food you swine' she said. Nobody moved. She stamped her foot. 'Food!' Well there we were with food before us and somebody gave her a dish of potatoes. She looked at it and then in a high, imperious voice like the shriek of an eagle: 'Not enough!' Everybody laughed at that, it was so typical you see of everything that we had done with. But suddenly she stooped, and when she rose we understood that she had set her food before the dogs. At that there was a roar of anger —there were plenty of children who needed food—and she and her dogs were bundled out without much ceremony. Her name was Countess Kretilinsky and later that day she drowned herself. I half expected Comrade Lenin to dismiss the tale as unimportant. But I remember that it made him silent. And after a little 'Hmp' he said 'Those people are having a very bad time'. And after a little again 'Hmp' He said 'History is hard'. History was mercilessly hard on Russia in those post-war years. With the end of the war came civil

war, and with the civil war came famine. By the Spring of
Nineteen Twenty, Russia was living hand to mouth.

He goes. Lights up. Zhelnik *enters unsteady.* Kollontai
comes after him agitated.

Kollontai: Fedor, come away.

Zhelnik: Shurrup. *(He roars)* Where is he?

Krupskaya *enters with a cloth-covered tray.*

Krupskaya: Fedor?

Kollontai: Oh Nadezhda . . .

Krupskaya: What's the matter? Comrade? Are you drunk?

Zhelnik: Drunk enough.

Krupskaya: Alexandra Mihailovna. How dare you bring him
here? This evening Vladya has a public meeting, two
Committees and—

Zhelnik: —Never stops does he?

Krupskaya: No he doesn't—!

Lenin *enters, briskly, unbuttoning his overcoat, but
checks:*

Kollontai: I'm sorry, Vladya, Fedor's drunk.

Zhelnik: 'S' righ'.

Lenin: Comrade, you're a fool . . .

Zhelnik: Never said I wasn't.

Lenin: You used to be a revolutionary.

Zhelnik: Right. Kronstadt Sailor. Don't you forget it.

Kollontai: He doesn't know what he's saying, Vladya.

Zhelnik: Shrrup—! Bourgeois bitch . . .

*But he looks round at her and she goes to him and puts
her hand on his shoulder.*

Lenin: You've been working too hard, Fedor. You'd better
take a rest.

Zhelnik: Work?

Lenin: Vital work.

Zhelnik: You don't know anything, do you? . . . Look . . .
Oh what's the good . . .

Lenin: Go on.

Zhelnik: We come to this village. We say 'Comrades, we hear
that you have grain'. They day 'No, we haven't.' Usual. So
we find the grain; there's half a barn full. We say
'Comrades, we must take this grain for the starving workers'.

69

They say 'Let 'em starve.' Usual. So we start to load the grain. And somebody sets fire to it. Gone in five minutes, barn and all. And so, we . . . shoot them. Men, women, kids. We shoot them.

      Lenin *takes out a notebook and pencil.*

Lenin: Who was in charge of the detachment?

Zhelnik: I was.

Lenin: *You* were?

Zhelnik: Ah—but we have this Chekist with us. And the Cheka's always in charge, isn't it?

Lenin: The Cheka takes precedence, yes.

Zhelnik: Oh he took that all right. He says 'Comrades we're going to make an example here.' He says, it's a nest of counter-revolution. We're going to show them what Red Terror means!

Lenin: Well?

Zhelnik: They were peasants!

Lenin: A peasant can be counter-revolutionary. Many of them are.

Zhelnik: Vladimir Ilyich—I'm a peasant! My brothers are peasants! We're all—*peasants!*

Lenin: Look. They burned the grain.

Zhelnik: They burned it, yes—

Lenin: —and the Revolution needs it?

Zhelnik: —Yes but—

Lenin: —Then what they did was counter-revolutionary.

Zhelnik: They weren't thinking about *that!*

Lenin: No. No I don't suppose they were. But if you *act* against the Revolution, then—no matter what you *think*— you are in fact a counter-revolutionary.

Zhelnik: Children?

      Lenin's *face goes drab for a beat. Then:*

Lenin: We shot the children of the Tsar, did you object to that?

Zhelnik: That was different.

Lenin: Why was it different?

Zhelnik: Well perhaps it wasn't so bloody different!

Lenin: Are you a Tsarist?

Zhelnik: I'd have shot the Tsar myself!

Lenin: The moment that the Tsar was dead, the little Tsaravich became the Tsar. It's not a matter of guilt; it's a matter of necessity.

> **Zhelnik** *growls; the women look unhappy.*

What was the name of this Chekist?

Zhelnik: Shatki; he's a Lithuanian jew.

Lenin: What's that got to do with it?

Zhelnik: Nothing.

Lenin: Do you want to be put on different work?

Zhelnik: I want to go back to Kronstadt.

Lenin: Very well.

> *He puts away the notebook.* **Zhelnik** *gets up unsteadily.*
> **Kollontai** *goes with him.* **Lenin** *watching them:*

Lenin: I'm disappointed in you, Comrade.

Zhelnik: Well . . . I'm sorry.

> *He goes, with* **Kollontai.** **Lenin** *broods.* **Krupskaya** *takes the cloth from the tray; a glass of milk, sandwiches.*

Krupskaya: Vladya . . .

Lenin: I'm not hungry.

Krupskaya: Eat, man.

> *Abstractedly he obeys. She watches him.*

He was drunk Vladya.

Lenin: He wasn't so drunk . . . *(He swallows; agreeably surprised:)*

What's this?

Krupskaya: Goose.

Lenin: Goose?

Krupskaya: Some peasants came and left it for you. Eat.

Lenin: Get me some cheese.

Krupskaya: Oh for goodness sake—They left a whole barrow load—Everyone got one.

Lenin: What?

Krupskaya: People are concerned about you Vladya; me among them. Eat.

Lenin: Are you—*(his voice is thick)*—Are you telling me that Leading Comrades—here in this building—are getting more than the ration?

Krupskaya: Occasionally. *(He whips out the notebook again and scribbles)* I gave one to the janitor.

Lenin: Oh you gave one to the janitor. What noble

71

condescension. Nadya, did none of them refuse?

Krupskaya: Dzerzhinsky sent his to the common canteen.

Lenin: The rest of them should be cleaning gutters.

He rises, buttoning his coat.

Krupskaya: Well I shall eat it.

Lenin: I hope it chokes you.

Krupskaya: It's a gift!

Lenin: It's tribute!

Blackout.

A white spot falls vertically.

In it: **Fanya Kaplan**, *white-faced, carrying a heavy handbag. She calls:*

Kaplan: Comrade Lenin!

He joins her.

Lenin: Comrade?

Kaplan: My name is Fanya Kaplan. I am a member of th Peasant Revolutionary Party.

Lenin: Oh yes? *(He looks at his watch)*

Kaplan: We have been excluded from the Soviets.

Lenin: Yes, very properly.

Kaplan: All Parties but yours are excluded from the Soviets.

Lenin: Have you specific business, Comrade?—

Kaplan: I have a petition.

Lenin: Very well.

He holds out his hand while she unclasps her handbag but, pausing:

Kaplan: The Tsar used to accept petitions.

Lenin: Yes.

Kaplan: How does it feel?

Lenin: Depends on the petition.

Kaplan: This is my petition.

She pulls a pistol from the bag and fires. He cries out and reels away into the dark. She steps after him and gets off one more shot before Chekists rush on and seize her.

Lights up. Lenin has gone; Dzerzhinsky sits at the table. He wears a black leather coat. He speaks, without passion.

Dzerzhinsky: Fanya Kaplan, you are charged with wounding and attempting to assassinate V. I. Lenin, Chairman of the Council of People's Commissars. Do you admit this action?

Kaplan: I do.

Dzerzhinsky: Do you regret this action?

Kaplan: I bitterly regret that it was not successful.

Dzerzhinsky: The sentence is death.

Kaplan: Long live the Revolution!

> *The* **Chekists** *take her out.* **Dzerzhinsky** *takes his glasses off, presses his finger tips to his eyes, puts back his glasses and reads from a paper.*

Dzerzhinsky: Comrades of the Cheka. I have just received by wireless telegraph a message from the Volga Front where L. D. Trotsky, Commissar for War has taken personal command. The so-called Czeck Brigade, the Peasant Revolutionary, Menshevik and other White Guard forces have arrested Soviet officials and commenced a counter-revolutionary insurrection. English, French and American armies occupy Archangel, Vladivostock and Murmansk. White Guard bands command the Urals, and the Don. Savinkov's Brigade of Officers is ninety miles from Moscow. Yudenich occupies the heights of Petrograd. Thus, the attempt upon the life of V. I. Lenin is revealed as part of a co-ordinated effort to destroy the Revolution. An essential element of Revolution is Revolutionary Terror. And just as the Red Army in its battles cannot pause to see that no-one who is individually innocent is harmed, neither can the Cheka pause to establish individual guilt. Class guilt is sufficient guilt. From the Officer caste and from the bourgeoisie take hostages, representative and in large numbers. The slightest sign of opposition must be crushed by merciless mass execution. Hooligans also, looters, drunkards and curfew-breakers in particular are likewise to be executed, on the spot. Chekists, strike. He who flinches, he who wavers, he who pauses to indulge in legalistic scruples is himself an agent of the enemy and should be so regarded. Long live the Revolution. Long live the Red Revolutionary Terror.

> *He stares at nothing, lifeless.* **Lunacharsky** *enters and approaches. Quietly, as to an invalid:*

Lunacharsky: Vladya asked me to come and see you.

Dzerzhinsky: Oh yes . . .

> *He finds some papers.* **Lunacharsky** *sits.*

Lunacharsky: How terrible everything is, Felix.

Dzerzhinsky: We shall win in the end.

Lunacharsky: Yes . . . Felix, did you think that it would be so terrible? In Capri did you think so?

> **Dzerzhinsky** *looks at him and, very deliberate:*

Dzerzhinsky: I was never in Capri.

Lunacharsky: I envy you . . .

> **Dzerzhinsky** *looks at him again and finds it necessary to stand up and move away, with the papers.*

Dzerzhinsky: Comrade Lunacharsky, certain serious short comings in your work have been drawn to the attention of the Cheka.

Lunacharsky: What—?

Dzerzhinsky: For example: In the year commencing January 1920—

Lunacharsky: One moment! *(The gentle man is dreadfully angry. He collects himself)* One moment . . . My work, of all work has nothing to do with the Cheka.

Dzerzhinsky: Is it not Party work?

Lunacharsky: I am a Party Member and therefore all my work is Party work.

Dzerzhinsky: The Cheka's only work—is to enforce the Party's will. It was you more than anybody who persuaded me to undertake it. *(He returns to the paper)* In January 1920 your Commissariat indented for nine million pairs of children's shoes. This figure was unrealistic but—

Lunacharsky: It was not unrealistic. It was minimal.

Dzerzhinsky: It was judged to be unrealistic by the Politburo of the Party. Which did however authorize you to obtain five hundred and fifty thousand pairs. But by January 1921 you had secured no more than half that number. Why?

Lunacharsky: What?

Dzerzhinsky: You failed in your assignment Comrade. Why?

Lunacharsky: I failed, my dear Edmundovich, because those few remaining factories which are producing shoes are not producing children's shoes—but boots for the Red Army! . . You have a nice pair of boots yourself I notice.

Dzerzhinsky: I need them. Someone in your Commissariat appears to have his feet up.

Lunacharsky: Do you mean myself?

Dzerzhinsky: I don't yet know the culprit.

Lunacharsky: 'Culprit'?

Dzerzhinsky: When there is a failure there is either negligence or sabotage.

Lunacharsky: What utter and disgusting rubbish. When that idiotic woman came so close to killing Vladya, there was failure in the Cheka.

Dzerzhinsky: The culprits have been punished.

Lunacharsky: Well, there are no culprits in my Commissariat and no-one will be punished.

Dzerzhinsky: You are satisfied by failure?

Lunacharsky: I am satisfied by effort.

Dzerzhinsky: By insufficient effort.

Lunacharsky: By maximum effort!

Dzerzhinsky: If your people are making a maximum effort your people are incompetent. And you are the culprit.

Lunacharsky: They are people most of whom it is a privilege to work with; most of whom are working fourteen hours a day —in conditions which defy description!

Dzerzhinsky: And yet they failed.

Lunacharsky: And yet they failed. Precisely.

Dzerzhinsky: The failure should have been reported.

Lunacharsky: It was repeatedly reported.

> **Dzerzhinsky** *looks at him and sits, takes up a pencil ready to make notes.*

Dzerzhinsky: By whom, and to whom?

Lunacharsky: By the Head of the Section for nursery education to the Head of the relevant section at the Commissariat for Clothing.

Dzerzhinsky: Can you tell me the dates of these representations?

Lunacharsky: Off hand of course I can't.

Dzerzhinsky: Please submit a memorandum.

Lunacharsky: Right. And now if we have come to the limits of your sudden interest in education—*(He makes to go)*

Dzerzhinsky: We have not.

> **Dzerzhinsky** *gets up again; he seems now almost nervous.*

75

Last year, at your request, sixteen hundred children were
evacuated from the famine districts of the Volga.

    Lunacharsky *goes still. Quietly.*

Lunacharsky: Yes?

Dzerzhinsky: How many of those children have you under care?

Lunacharsky: It's hard to say. They run away.

Dzerzhinsky: And then?

Lunacharsky: You know as well as I what then. They run about
like starving dogs.

Dzerzhinsky: And starving dogs are dangerous; there have been
incidents . . . which—

Lunacharsky: I don't need to be told about the incidents.

Dzerzhinsky: I have been instructed to gather up these children
and return them to the Volga.

Lunacharsky: . . . I warn you Comrade, this I shall protest.

    Dzerzhinsky *smiles a little.*

Dzerzhinsky: There is no need to warn me Anatole Vassilyevich.
In fact, speaking personally—

Lunacharsky: —D'you remember how to speak, personally?

    Dzerzhinsky's *face goes stiff again.*

Dzerzhinsky: A timely warning. Thank you. That is all.

    Lunacharsky *rises, going.* **Dzerzhinsky,** *collecting up his
papers says to his receding back:*

You will use the proper channels for your protest, Comrade.

Lunacharsky: I will protest this from the housetops.

Dzerzhinsky: Be careful. Comrade.

    It is a warning, a friendly threat. But **Lunacharsky** *goes
back to him, stands threateningly close and, warningly:*

Lunacharsky: No Felix Edmundovich. *You* be careful!

    *They go, in opposite directions. Light change and
Sailors, Soldiers, Workers and one Clerk enter, with
Zhelnik who sits at the table and takes up a pen,
clumsily, and says, a bit embarrassed but very earnest:*

Zhelnik: The Temporary Revolutionary Council of Sailors
Soldiers and Workers of Kronstadt is in session. Very well
Brothers.

A Sailor: Cheka.

    Angry and instant agreement.

2nd Sailor: Peasants.

> *Agreement the same.*

1st Worker: —Unions.

Clerk: Rations.

Soldier: —Elections.

Sailor: —The Party!

> *Angry agreement.* **Trotsky** *enters, opposite, and the chorus dies. He wears a uniform and boots. Regards them coldly. The* **Crowd** *looks to* **Zhelnik,** *who rises. A bit awed, but stubbornly and with menace.*

Zhelnik: These are the demands of the Kronstadt Council: One: Free canvassing for all genuinely revolutionary Parties.

Trotsky: No Party is so genuinely revolutionary as the Bolshevik Party. Therefore canvassing for other Parties is counter-revolutionary. Demand rejected.

Zhelnik: Two. Control of the factories by worker committees.

Trotsky: The factories now belong to the workers and committee control is unproductive. Demand rejected.

Zhelnik: Three: An end to methods of grain procurement which terrorize the peasantry. And freedom for the peasant to use his land as he thinks fit.

Trotsky: The land and its produce belong to the People. Demand rejected.

Zhelnik: Finally: The immediate release of all persons placed in prison by the Cheka, or the immediate review of all such cases by an elected, independent, non-Party commission.

Trotsky: As the Party to the People so the Cheka to the Party. Demand rejected.

Zhelnik: Right.

> **Zhelnik** *folds up the paper, looking firmly at* **Trotsky,** *who, dropping his official manner steps towards them with a warm and confident smile.*

Trotsky: Now Comrades listen—

> *They explode into an uproar of angry shouts, jeers and whistles. His face goes severe again. Suddenly the uproar dies and he looks round to see the cause of it.* **Kollontai** *has entered behind him. The* **Crowd** *falls back a bit from* **Zhelnik,** *embarrassed by the situation.*

Kollontai: Oh Fedor . . . Oh my dear—Don't you see . . . ?

Zhelnik *(growls):* See what?

Trotsky *(gently, sadly):* Come away, Alexia.

> *But she motions him back.*

Kollontai: Comrades do you think the Party does not understand? Do you think we do not know the Revolution has been stern, and dreadful . . .? *(Her voice breaks; she wipes her eyes impatiently and:)* But Comrades did we ever think it would be easy? Peaceful? Fair? Like a duel at dawn between two officers, with an umpire and a doctor standing by—and all sit down together afterwards for breakfast? No no. Revolution is a *real* fight. Naked as Nature. And cruel as Nature. And will you join the enemy? Fedor? Will you fight with the White Guard? Comrades, you have been duped . . .!

Zhelnik: We've been duped all right. But not by the White Guard.

> *The light begins to fail and distant guns are heard like soft drums.* **Trotsky** *reads a proclamation:*

Trotsky: To the Kronstadt rebels from the Worker-Peasant Government. Lay down your arms immediately. Release at once the commissars you have illegally arrested and submit yourselves to Revolutionary Justice. Simultaneous with this have ordered General Tukachevsky—

> *A stir among the* **Crowd.**

—to advance against you the Red Army. Only those who submit unconditionally can expect the mercy of the Soviet Republic. This warning is the last.

> *Guns louder, light darker; the* **Clerk** *steps forward.*

Clerk: Against you and General Tukachevsky we advance the bloodstained banner of the labouring people. We will stand or fall—in Kronstadt!

> *The guns roar, blackness falls.*

Kollontai: Fedor!

> *A flash and light change to green and dappled sunlight. The bellowing guns recede. Birdsong.* **Lenin** **Trotsky, Stalin, Krupskaya, Lunacharsky** *enter left* **Kollontai** *right. She wears black.* **Lenin** *glances at her under his brows as she sits, white-faced at the table. All sit. They have folders.* **Trotsky** *has a pile of folders.* **Lenin** *in speaks; his personality has darkened; he looks older.*

Lenin: The subject is Kronstadt. We will begin with the report from Comrade General Tukachevsky. It is of course completely confidential. Will someone read it—?—I would like to save my voice.

Kollontai: I will read it.

   Lenin *momentarily startled. Then:*

Lenin: Very well.

   Kollontai *reads, with an effort, but clearly:*

Kollontai: He says: 'In five continuous years of war I cannot remember such a slaughter. Our heavy artillery began on March 7th and was so heavy that windows were shattered as far away as Orenbaum. The sailors fought like wild beasts. I cannot understand where they found such fury. Each house where they were located had to be taken by storm. An entire company fought for an hour to occupy one house and suffered heavy losses. It had been held against them by three sailors armed with hand-grenades and one machine-gun. It was not until the evening of the seventeenth that all resistance was overcome. Long live the Revolution'.

   They stir.

Lenin: The subject is Kronstadt. Suggest—

   Gorky *enters. A confrontation.*

Who let you in?

Krupskaya: I did, Vladya.

Lenin: What d'you want?

Gorky: I want to go back to Capri.

Lenin: Sit down.

Gorky: Vladya, I don't—

Lenin: —Sit down . . . And listen.

   As **Gorky** *sits apart:*

The subject is Kronstadt. Propose Comrade Trotsky to lead the discussion.

   Trotsky *leans forward, eager to begin.*

Kollontai: Propose Comrade Lenin to lead the discussion.

Stalin: Agree.

Trotsky: Very well.

Lenin: Get on. What does it matter who leads—? *(He squints painfully and pinches the bridge of his nose)* —Get on.

   Gorky *looks at him.*

Trotsky: The Kronstadt rising forces us to face a seemingly impossible event. The Revolutionary vanguard turns upon the Revolution. Why?

Kollontai: Because the Revolution turned on them.

Stalin: In my analysis the Kronstadt mutiny resulted from the discontent; aroused in petty-bourgeois elements; by White Guard agitation.

> *The platitudes come from him woodenly.* **Trotsky** *explains, condescending.*

Trotsky: Successful agitation presupposes discontent. Now—

Dzerzhinsky: There was agitation.

Trotsky: No doubt there was—

Stalin: Well then?

Trotsky: Look. May I get on?

Stalin: Oh. Sorry.

> **Trotsky** *sits back and:*

Trotsky: Comrade Stalin will lead the discussion.

> **Lenin** *hits the table with the flat of his hand.*

Krupskaya: Lead, Vladya.

Lunacharsky: Yes.

Lenin: Right.

> **Trotsky** *displeased and isolated.*

They did not turn upon the revolution. They turned upon the Party. And they turned upon the State. Because the Party and the State are rotten with bureaucracy and we are rotten with conceit.

> *They are surprised and excited.* **Gorky** *cocks his head.*

We are moreover criminally ignorant. We know the proletariat; perhaps. Inside the Commissariats we know every corridor and cupboard. Of the peasant, we know nothing. And all he knows of us is this: that we expropriate. What more could he know? The average peasant cannot read. And we pay him with a pamphlet when we drive away his pig. We tell him we must have his harvest for the 'World Revolution'. To him the revolution is an empty barn, and the world outside his parish is a dubious abstraction. He finds our motives unintelligible and our actions only too familiar. Kronstadt rose against us as it rose against the landlords. And we like any landlord have the impudence to be surprised.

Gorky *has turned right round in his chair.* **Lenin,** *sourly:*

I thought you might be interested.

He turns back to the others.

Therefore, we propose the immediate dissolution of the grain procurement squads.

Kollontai: Hallelulia . . .

Lunacharsky: Well—

Lenin: Mp?

Lunacharsky: Well—Hallelulia, yes—I hate the grain procurement squads. But we do have to procure it . . .

Lenin: Yes. *(To* Trotsky*)* Go on.

Trotsky: Each peasant will continue to deliver to the State a percentage of his annual harvest. The rest he will be free to sell.

Lunacharsky: Free?

Trotsky: Yes.

Lunacharsky: But, do you mean that he will sell to anybody who can buy?

Trotsky: Yes.

Lunacharsky: Sell at a profit—?—And?—The weak to the wall?

Trotsky: A market economy. Yes.

Dzerzhinsky: But—forgive me Leon Davidovich—but it seems to me that what you are proposing is capitalist enterprise.

Trotsky: Yes.

Stalin: Then what you are proposing is counter-revolution.

Trotsky looks up slowly, then quickly at Stalin. *It seems he will explode. But:*

Trotsky: What we are proposing is a limited admission of capitalist enterprise contained within the context of the Socialist State.

Stalin: A capitalist economy necessitates a bourgeois State.

Trotsky: You've been studying your Marxist primer. Advance now if you will to the study of the dialectic.

Lenin: Stop it! The dialectic is a two-edged weapon, Leon. It is possible to cut yourself.

Trotsky: What is that supposed to mean?

They confront for a moment. Lenin *decides to wait till later.*

Comrade Stalin's point is exceedingly well taken. Of course there will be every kind of vile attack upon the Party and the State from the racketeers and speculators who will now come out of hiding. But it does not follow that the Party and the State must weaken. It follows that the Party must tighten its grip on the State. And the Party must be purged.

Lunacharsky: Purged?

Lenin: Mp? Yes. Now Leon.

Lunacharsky: Just a minute. In what sense 'purged'?

Trotsky: It is a medical expression, Anatole Vassilyevich, signifying the excretion by an organism of whatever is corrupt.

Dzerzhinsky: Corrupt!

Trotsky: I don't of course mean personal corruption, corruption in the bourgeois sense of taking bribes and things like that. I mean institutional corruption. *(He is finding a file from the pile beside him).*

Lunacharsky: I don't like the distinction, Leon. Institutions are composed of persons.

Trotsky: For example, that admirable institution, the Commissariat for Education is institutionally and objectively corrupt precisely because you are personally, subjectively and if I may say so excessively innocent.

Lunacharsky: Then you'd better get rid of me.

Trotsky: Quite possibly. At all events we must erect an organ of the Party to inspect the Commissariats without fear or favour and with power to make appointments and dismissals on the spot.

Lunacharsky: An organ of the Party?

Trotsky: A Commission of Inspection, yes.

    Lunacharsky *throws up his hands.*

Lunacharsky: I simply do not understand.

Lenin: What don't you understand?

Lunacharsky: He says the rot is instituional and then he says we'll cure it with another institution! It's more bureaucracy—not less!

Trotsky: And how would you propose to cure it?

Lunacharsky: With more sincerity and self-denial!

Trotsky: Disembodied?

Kollontai: Embodied in sincere and self-denying persons, Leon

Trotsky: I expect to find such persons in the organs of the Party.

Kollontai: And do you—?—Always?

Trotsky: No. *(He flips open another dossier)* The Party is an institution too.

Stalin: The Party is an 'institution'?

Trotsky: It is not an idea in somebody's head. Marx—as I am sure you know—believed in a material reality.

> *He has another file, and this one has a lock on it. He opens it and drops the tone of donnish banter.*

The Party of the proletariat is not of course an institution just like any other. In the year before the Revolution when there was nothing much to gain by Membership and everything to lose we had at most ten thousand active Members. We have a hundred thousand paid Officials now. And three-quarters of a million Members. Half of whom are not much more than middle-class careerists. There are actually paid officials who were members of the old bureaucracy. The Party has been interpenetrated by reactionary elements.

> **Lunacharsky** *shows unease.*

I am not saying Anatole that all these people know themselves to be reactionary. Some of them perhaps in all sincerity believe themselves to be converted. But they are helplessly imbued with a bureaucratic and reactionary turn of mind. And the Party must expel them—Yes—even though they may not know themselves for what, objectively they are.

Lenin: Correct!

Lunacharsky: But if they do not know themselves—how the devil can we *know* them?

Gorky: *Good!*

Lenin *(whirls and points at him):* You were told that you could listen, not that you could speak. The local Secretaries know them.

Lunacharsky: But if we're looking for careerists it's just the Local Secretaries that we're likely to be looking for!

Trotsky: We will begin with the Local Secretaries.

Lunacharsky: 'We' will—? Who will?

Trotsky: The Central Secretariat.

Lunacharsky: And who will purge the Central Secretariat—?—The Cheka?

Trotsky: Yes.

Lunacharsky: And—? . . . Leon, it's an endless regress!

Lenin (*suddenly, loudly, heavily, angrily*): Why 'endless'?

Gorky: Why? Good Heavens can't you see? It's as ancient as the hills—!—Who will guard the Guardians?—Plato's problem—D'you think you're going to solve it with a Party directive?

Lenin: Yes. Plato was a slave-owning idealist, so his Republic needed perfect men. Our Republic needs Party men.

Gorky: You said the Party was corrupt.

Lenin: Honest Party men.

Gorky: Diogenes looked for an honest man—with a lighted lamp at noon.

Lenin: And he probably passed a dozen men more honest than himself. A man who insists on impossible standards isn't an ethical paragon—he's an ethical clown—!—Like you—! —Be *quiet* . . .!

He gasps and frowns and pinches the bridge of his nose.

Krupskaya: Vladya?

Lenin: All right. (*To* **Lunacharsky**) Now—to identify a Party man we do not need a 'lamp at noon'. We need the following objective facts: when did he become a Member, what has he been doing since, from what class-background did he come. We need these facts in a written record, accurate and up to date. It's going to be a colossal job. Mechanical and never-ending, unrewarding and unsung.

Stalin: And so we'll offer it to Comrade Stalin. Unless I miss my guess.

Lenin: We know that he's a Party man already; from his record.

Stalin: I think you mean a Party functionary.

Kollontai: We're all Party functionaries, Josef.

      Stalin *is gathering up his papers, dark faced.*

Stalin: Oh no. Oh no. Some of us are Party leaders.

Lenin: Do you accept or not?

      Stalin *pauses, looks at him under his brows.*

Stalin: You say you know my record. When did I refuse?

      He goes back to collecting up his papers, slapping files one on another by way of punctuation.

I've been a bandit for the Party. A soldier for the Party. I've

84

washed dishes for the Party. If the Party wants a Clerk all right I'll be a Party clerk.

He squares up his folders and heavily but steadily, impersonal but stern.

Lenin: Thank you—

Stalin *hasn't finished.*

Stalin: But it is absolutely obvious—that you and Comrade Trotsky met before this meeting and decided what it should decide. Thus violating the collective leadership. Thus demonstrating your contempt for the collective leadership. This cult of individual leaders, this reliance upon individual ability, is basically incorrect. I condemn this practice. I censure this practice. I demand that it cease.

Lenin: I accept your censure. I second your demand.

Stalin: In the period confronting us—it seems to me—that Party unity must be maintained, at any cost whatever.

Lenin: Now that's the most important thing that has been said by anyone today. I'd like to end this session there.

Lunacharsky: Well I—

Krupskaya: —Vladya's tired.

Lunacharsky: Are you?

Lenin: A little.

Lunacharsky: Very well.

They rise, gathering up their things.

Dzerzhinsky: Can we meet tomorrow?

Lenin: What? This evening if you like.

Krupskaya: Tomorrow.

They are going. However, **Kollontai** *crosses to* **Gorky.** *She kisses him on the forehead.*

Kollontai: Don't leave us Alexey.

She and **Lunacharsky** *go.*

Lenin: Yosef. It really is a most important job.

Stalin: I'm not blind, Vladya. It's a job for a mediocrity.

He goes, with **Dzerzhinsky.**

Trotsky: Then we've got the right man for it.

Gorky: Have you?

Trotsky: Oh come, be fair. Comrade Stalin's mediocrity is really quite exceptional.

Lenin: Bonaparte was witty too.

Trotsky: What?

Lenin: I say—

Trotsky: I heard what you said, Vladya. What did you mean?

Lenin: Have you a minute?

Trotsky: I have indeed. *(He sits, quietly)*

Lenin: You are by head and shoulders the most able person in the Party.

Trotsky: I'm terribly sorry; what ought I to do about it?

Lenin: You could be less aware of it. It doesn't put you above the Party.

Trotsky: I'm getting a bit sick of this.

Lenin: You've heard it before then.

Trotsky: Well of course I have . . . Do you believe it?

Lenin: What?

Trotsky: That I put myself above the Party; that I am the potential Bonaparte.

Lenin: I don't know a more likely candidate.

Trotsky: Have you thought of yourself?

Lenin: I've been too busy.

Trotsky: You have done no more than me.

Lenin: I haven't done as much as you; but I've been more fully occupied; it's taken all of me to do it. There's a bit of you to spare. Hand it over. Eh?

> **Trotsky** *looks at him. Steadily:*

Trotsky: Vladya, if you think that I may use the Army, to commandeer the Party and arrest the Revolution, you ought to have me shot. *(He is very serious)*

Lenin: Well I'm sure that's very handsome. But if I found myself believing that any individual could change the course of history, I wouldn't have him shot. I'd go and study my Marxist primer.

> **Trotsky** *doesn't smile. He is mentally winded. Gets up and goes.*

Now don't go and shoot yourself, there's a good chap.

> **Trotsky** *gone.* **Lenin** *looks after him, thoughtful and a shade worried.*

Gorky: Why did you do that?

Lenin: Mp?

Gorky: You've castrated him.

86

Lenin *gives it a moment's thought.*

Lenin: Rubbish.

But looks after **Trotsky** *again. Then:*

Needed trimming anyway. Too well equipped by half . . . Well, it's been a long time.

Gorky: Yes.

Lenin: Are you well?

Gorky: All right. Are you?

Lenin hesitates. Then, gloomily—it is not an admission he would make to anybody else:

Lenin: No I'm not. I've still got one of that bloody woman's bullets in me.

He works his shoulder irritably.

Lenin: Did you know her?

Gorky: No.

Lenin: Well. A brawl. People do what they must.

Gorky: Do they?

Lenin looks at him alert.

Lenin: Yes.

Gorky: Vladya, if she'd been a better shot, who would be sitting where you're sitting now?

Lenin smiles at him affectionately, gives him up and looks away and murmurs:

Lenin: This foolish friend of mine believes, in spite of all he's seen, that history goes the way it does because some hero's what he is.

Gorky: You are a modest megalomaniac. *(He rises)* And I want to go back to Capri.

Lenin: You want to go a good deal further back than that Alexey, don't you?

Gorky pulls three sealed envelopes out of his pocket.

Gorky: This is a list of innocent and useful people imprisoned without trial. They include the Menshevik Tsertelli. This is a list of people who may or may not have been innocent. They were executed by the Cheka. And this is a list of personal friends who have simply disappeared.

He is too moved to speak for a moment, shifts aimlessly and then, rounding on **Lenin***:*

You promised us new life, release, refinements, unimaginable forms. And all you have released is atavistic envy. There is no novelty whatever in your revolution, Vladya; no love, nor life, nor hope, nor even curiosity. It is merely ferocious.

Lenin: 'Merely' ferocious?

Gorky: You're proud of that?

Lenin: Yes.

Gorky: Complacently ferocious. This country always was barbaric but by God before the revolution, at least it was ashamed!

Lenin: You were ashamed—your sort was ashamed.—Look at him! The celebrated good, well-paid bad conscience— *(He sweeps the papers to the floor)* of the *shits*—that made us shameful! That's why you've turned against the Revolution, Alexey Maximovich—It's done you out of a job!

 Gorky going, furious. And this time he will go.

Alexey.

 Gorky stops, hesitates, turns square. **Lenin** *retrieves one of the papers.*

Would you stay if we let you publish?

Gorky: You wouldn't. Not what I want to print.

 Lenin *retrieves a second paper.*

Lenin: How far would you want to go?

Gorky: Oh well beyond your tolerance; I'd want to print the truth.

Lenin: Mp . . . No I couldn't let you publish that . . .

 He stoops and retrieves the last of the papers.

You're right. There's a lot of envy . . . And precious little love . . . But you seem to think that it's somebody's fault!

Gorky: I think it's your fault, Vladya.

Lenin: Yes I know you do. *(He sits with the papers)* And I'm damned if I see how a sensible man can think anything so silly . . .!

 He takes one of the lists in his hand, preparing to unfold it. Looking at no-one delivers his credo:

It is the passion of the masses which dictates the nature of the day. Sometimes the masses have no passion, and then the days are dead. But when it takes the form of envy, then envy is the form of life. We have no right to embrace our enemies, today, Alexey.

Gorky: I am not asking you to embrace enemies—

Lenin: Aren't you?

Gorky: No. I'm asking for a bit of necessary tolerance—For people like Tsertelli. He's not a White Guard Officer. He's a Left of Centre Socialist.

Lenin: A well to the left of Centre Socialist, and an honourable man.

Gorky: Yes!

Lenin: But if I am allowed to tolerate him he has a right to be tolerant too. And he's admirably tolerant—like every Left of Centre Socialist. He would embrace a White Guard. Oh yes he would—!—Catch him after a good dinner, with a tolerant White Guard. And who wouldn't *he* embrace? *(He sighs, but firmly, as a challenge:)* One step leads to another. And any step now is forward or back.

Gorky: And this is the way forward?

Lenin: Yes.

Gorky: I want to go back.

　　　　Lenin turns away from him.

Lenin: Go then.

Gorky: May I take Ekaterina?

Lenin: What? Yes.

Gorky: Who shall I see?

Lenin: See anyone!

　　　　Gorky *goes.* **Lenin** *rubs his forehead, squinting painfully. Pulls a typewritten list from the envelope.* **Lunacharsky** *enters and stands looking at him.* **Lenin** *squints at the paper, holds it away from him, looks up at the light, puzzled.*

Lenin: Can you read this?

　　　　Lunacharsky *doesn't move. From where he stands, sadly:*

Lunacharsky: Yes.

Lenin: I can't. *(Looks round puzzled)* I can't see anything clearly . . . *(He rises unsteadily)* Wah . . .!

Lunacharsky *(quietly):* What?

Lenin: I've got the most amazing headache . . . I hope I'm not going to be ill.

　　　　He goes.

89

Lunacharsky: We did not know it at the time but Comrade Lenin's amazing headache was the onset of the cerebral atrophy which as of course you know first incapacitated him, and two years later, took him from us. *(He clears his throat, smiles painfully and:)* Excuse me. The political loss was of course incalculable. But the personal loss was more immediate.

> **Krupskaya** *enters. Forcedly calm.*

Krupskaya: 'Tolly will you come? Vladya appears to be quite unwell.

Lunacharsky: Wha—?

Krupskaya: 'Tolly—He can't speak.

> *They go. Hot sunlight.* **Chekists** *enter with* **Mdvani**. *They thrust him into a chair. Then one goes and arranges a table to confront him. He attempts to get up. The other* **Chekist** *thrusts him down into the chair again.* **Stalin** *enters; he is carrying a folder and smoking the famous pipe. He takes this from his mouth and stops short, surprised.*

Stalin: What's this?

> **Chekists** *bewildered. He gives an indulgent laugh and tells them amicably:*

Get out you fools.

> *They go. As apologizing for a ludicrous faux pas:*

Sorry, Victor.

Mdvani: Drop it, Josef. I remember you.

Stalin: Well I should hope you do remember me. *(He seems a little hurt)* Remember the Tiflis bank raid?

Mdvani: Yes. I remember that you were in Baku.

Stalin: Victor, I am not here to settle old accounts.

Mdvani: I know why you're here; it's a joke.

Stalin: Why do you say that?

Mdvani: I've told you, Josef, I remember you. You're here to clean up the Georgean Party. I wouldn't use you to pull through a sewer.

> **Stalin** *looks at him a moment. Then:*

Stalin: Very well. What is this?

> *He shows him some small sheets of closely written paper.*

Mdvani: That's a personal letter from me to my wife.

Stalin: Yes. Do you remember what's in it?

Mdvani: Comradely criticism is perfectly legitimate.

Stalin: Comradely . . . V. I. Lenin is *(reads)* 'a paralytic theologan who ought to be retired', Comrade Zinoviev 'a Jewish cretin, Lenin's bootlicker', Comrade Lunacharsky is 'a neuresthenic nanny', I am described as 'a back-street lout' and Comrade Kollontai is 'a randy old librarian with her brains between her legs'.

Mdvani: Look. It's a private letter. Matter of fact I was pissed when I wrote it.

Stalin: Humorous exaggeration.

Mdvani: Yes!

Stalin: Mm. Well none of this much matters because this is pettily personal. But do you remember what you said about the whole collective leadership?

Mdvani: No.

Stalin: No?

Mdvani: Not exactly.

Stalin: 'A gang of greater Russian military chauvinists, no better than the Tsar . . .'

> He underlines the last five words so that they hang heavily in the silence.

Mdvani: Did you get that letter from Natasha?

Stalin: No. Pratkov got it. From Natasha.

Mdvani: Pratkov! So Moscow has suborned the Georgean Cheka to spy on the Georgean Central Committee. You bloody, clumsy fool. D'you think you can get away with that?

Stalin: I don't see that it's anything to get away with Victor.

Mdvani: We'll see what Party Conference thinks.

Stalin: It seems to me that nobody who thinks like this ought to be at Party Conference.

Mdvani: There's nothing you can do about it. Delegations aren't appointed from the Centre, they're elected by the Party here.

Stalin: But I am here to purge your Party.

> **Mdvani** *stares appalled, beginning to understand, beginning perhaps to guess the future.* **Dzerzhinsky** *enters, also with a file; he is poker-faced and quietly*

certain of his purpose. Sits by **Stalin.**

Mdvani: Felix Edmundovich—I wish to make a formal protest—!—

Dzerzhinsky: Please sit down. *(To* **Stalin***)* How far have you got?

> **Stalin** *passes him the letter.*

Mdvani: That document was stolen.

Dzerzhinsky: It is a criminal document, Comrade Mdvani. *(He places it neatly in the file, pedantic and calm as a clerk)* I have some questions for you, Comrade.

Mdvani: Where is my wife?

> **Dzerzhinsky** *hesitates, then:*

Dzerzhinsky: Your wife is at home.

> **Mdvani** *rubs his hand over his face.* **Dzerzhinsky,** *irritated by his own weak-mindedness:*

Now I have some questions for you.

> **Mdvani** *sits back and signifies his readiness.*

Dzerzhinsky: In the matter of the integration of the Trans-caucasian Republics—

Mdvani: Yes?

Dzerzhinsky: What have you done?

Mdvani: We have discussed it with the Party of Armenia. Several times.

Dzerzhinsky: And what emerged from these discussions?

Mdvani: That neither Party wanted it.

Dzerzhinsky: According to the Armenians it was you who did not want it.

Mdvani: We have a saying about Armenians.

Dzerzhinsky: Doubtless. *(He makes a note)* You know of course that it is Party Policy that you should integrate.

> *This is the sticking point.* **Mdvani** *looks at him and takes a breath, before:*

Mdvani: We appeal from Party policy to the Soviet constitution.

> **Stalin** *looks up;* **Dzerzhinsky,** *cautiously:*

Dzerzhinsky: To which part of the Constitution?

Mdvani: The part which guarantees the national integrity of the National Republics.

Dzerzhinsky: It does not guarantee reaction in the guise of national integrity.

Mdvani: Reaction!

Dzerzhinsky: Three years ago you had in Georgia three collective farms. How many have you now?

Mdvani *(on a note of exasperated reiteration):* Felix Edmundovich, our peasants do not like collective farms. And our peasants here are not potato-eating Russians—they are Georgean mountaineers.

Dzerzhinsky: Do you wish me to record the phrase 'potato-eating Russians'?

Mdvani: . . . No . . . Thanks.

Dzerzhinsky: I am not here to trick or trap you Comrade; I am here to ascertain the truth. What do your peasants like?

Mdvani: Five acres and a fence.

Dzerzhinsky: And you are satisfied to let them have five acres and a fence.

Mdvani: 'Let' them . . . *(He gives a silent laugh)* My father was a peasant—

Dzerzhinsky: Was he a wealthy peasant?

Mdvani: Your father was a Polish noble—don't talk to me about wealth . . . He had one little field; it wasn't much of a field; it was a stony-hearted bitch of a field. But by God it had a good fence. He was half-insane about the field; he used to talk to it; he would have fucked it if he could I think. And there wasn't much he couldn't fuck . . . *(He is lost. But now he looks at* Dzerzhinsky*)* And he would certainly have killed you if you'd laid a finger on the fence.

Dzerzhinsky: So collectivization here is impossible.

Mdvani: Unless you want an all-out war between the Party and the peasants, yes.

> **Dzerzhinsky** *thinks a second, then gently and seriously like a doctor who begins to suspect his patient has cancer:*

Dzerzhinsky: In the event of such a war, on which side would we find you fighting, Victor?

> **Mdvani** *looks at him startled.*

Mdvani: I hope that's a hypothetical question.

Dzerzhinsky: It's your hypothesis.

Mdvani: I would be on the side of the masses.

Dzerzhinsky: The Party would be on the side of the masses.

93

Mdvani: In a war against the mass?

Dzerzhinsky: In any war.

Mdvani: Felix, is this contemplated?

Dzerzhinsky: Who knows what History contemplates?

> *He looks sad and dreamy, like a martyr envisaging his inevitable end. Then briskly:*

It is not contemplated policy. Current policy is to collectivize the peasants by persuasion and example.

Mdvani: Felix, I've been doing that!

Dzerzhinsky: No. I think perhaps you think you have. But I do not think you can. You do not speak of peasant farming as the beastly backward thing it is; you speak of it with sympathy and fellow-feeling; I think you speak of it with pride. You are drifting towards a separated Georgia based on petty private ownership and national intransigence. And that would be a rotten apple in the basket of the Soviet State.

> *This is political, perhaps actual death. He looks down unhappily.*

You joined the Party in the Spring of 1917.

Mdvani: Yes.

> **Dzerzhinsky** *makes a tick.*

Dzerzhinsky: Until that date you were a member of the Mensheviks.

Mdvani: Correct.

> **Dzerzhinsky** *makes another tick.*

Dzerzhinsky: Thank you.

Stalin: I have a question, Felix. May I have that letter? *(He glances at it, drawing at his pipe. Then:)* This isn't a question I want to ask. But we were told to work without fear or favour. And what we have uncovered here, objectively considered is conspiratorial, petty-bourgeois, counter revolutionary chauvinism. Now, the only member of the leadership who does not come in for your 'comradely criticism' appears to be Comrade Trotsky. Is he aware of your conspiracy?

> **Dzerzhinsky** *startled.* **Mdvani** *chuckles grimly.*

Mdvani: That question is 'conspiratorial'—*(Bitterly sarcastic)*—Comrade.

Dzerzhinsky *(uneasy):* I'm bound to say, Josef—

Stalin: Without fear or favour.

Dzerzhinsky: Answer the question.

Mdvani: All right. No, Comrade Trotsky is not aware of our petty-bourgeois, counter-revolutionary chauvinist conspiracy—

Dzerzhinsky: Thank you.

Mdvani: —He is aware of our legitimate aspirations.

Stalin: And what does he say about them?

Mdvani: He says they are chauvinistic, petty-bourgeois and counter-revolutionary.

Stalin: I expected no less of Comrade Trotsky.

Mdvani: By God you haven't changed.

> **Dzerzhinsky** *rises and, formal:*

Dzerzhinsky: Thank you, Comrade.

> **Mdvani** *rises.*

The honesty with which you have responded to my questions will be counted in your favour.

Mdvani: Dzerzhinsky . . . you're mad. *(He looks at* **Stalin***)* God knows what you are.

> *Going, he crosses* **Draganov,** *entering. Both stop.*

Mdvani: You bastard . . . You pig-shit. *(He goes)*

Dzerzhinsky: Comrade Pratkov?

Draganov *(clicks his heels):* Comrade.

Dzerzhinsky: One moment. *(Consults papers with* **Stalin***)* Draganov—

> *He turns.*

Draganov: Com— *(He realises his mistake too late)* Shit . . .

Dzerzhinsky: Captain Draganov; you are an agent.

Draganov: No.

Dzerzhinsky: Yes!

Draganov: For whom am I working?

Dzerzhinsky: You are working for the class to which you helplessly belong.

Draganov: It no longer exists.

Dzerzhinsky: You exist. You joined the Party under an assumed identity.

Draganov: Yes.

Dzerzhinsky: If you are not an agent, why?

Draganov: I wanted a Party Ration Card.

Dzerzhinsky: You are being very frank.

Draganov: Why not?

Dzerzhinsky: You also had the blasphemous temerity to join the Cheka.

Draganov: Yes.

Dzerzhinsky: Why did you do that?

> *Dzerzhinsky looks straight at him and, half claim, half apology.*

Draganov: It's my job.

> *Dzerzhinsky flushes.*

Dzerzhinsky: Give me your card; your papers. *(He tears them across)* Outside.

Stalin: Disgusting bourgeois cynicism. Shoot him.

Dzerzhinsky: Yes . . .

> *He rises with a sigh and says to* Chekist

See to that.

Chekist: Right.

> *Dzerzhinsky goes.* Stalin *gathering his things together,* Chekist *watching him alertly.*

Stalin: Does Comrade Mdvani know that you have monitored his telephone?

Chekist: No.

Stalin: Are you certain?

Chekist: Yes.

Stalin: Was it you who got this letter?

Chekist: Yes. It was my case.

Stalin: *How* did you get it?

Chekist: Does it matter?

Stalin: Perhaps not. *(He knocks out his pipe)* You seem to know your business, Comrade—er . . .

Chekist: Kuskow.

Stalin: Kuskow. Yes. Well it's as good a name as any. How long would you say you have been a policeman?

Chekist: I joined the Cheka in the year of its inception, Comrade.

Stalin: No previous experience?

Chekist: No Comrade.

Stalin: You must have natural aptitude. It's time you were promoted. Comrade.

> *He goes. Light change from Georgia to dappled sunlight.* Chekist *stands at ease. But snaps to attention*

as **Lenin** *enters. He walks with a stick, dragging his paralysed right arm and leg. He glowers at* **Chekist** *and speaks, thickly and with arbitrary jerks where his tongue refuses service.*

Lenin: Wh-o are y-ou?

Chekist: Yakolyev, Igor Borisovich.

Lenin: Where is F-ustnits-ky?

Chekist: Ordered onto other duties I believe, Comrade Lenin.

Lenin grunts. Then:

Lenin: Are you fer-om G-eorgia?

Chekist stares then laughs admiringly. **Lenin** *grunts, interrogative.*

Chekist: Yes I am from Georgia. I was wondering how you knew.

Lenin: I am cer-lairv-oyant.

Geutier, Kollontai, Krupskaya enter. He throws his good arm out and sideways. **Kollontai** *goes to him, stoops; they embrace. Then, over her back to* **Geutier:**

Lenin: Y-ou go a-way.

Geutier smiles, goes on taking things from his doctor's bag.

G-o away!

This is more serious. **Krupskaya** *pleadingly:*

Krupskaya: Vladya . . .

Lenin: What?

Krupskaya: Don't be troublesome . . .

Lenin: Not in a pos-ition to be ter-ter- *(He pauses, glaring into space)* ter- *(He pauses again. Raises his clenched fist and smashes it onto the table. Still nothing comes. Then:)* -roublesome!

The rage and resentment in it are frightening. **Kollontai** *bites her lip.* **Lenin** *fighting for breath.* **Geutier** *comes with a spoonful of medicine.*

Geutier: Ilyich.

Lenin: N-o.

Krupskaya: Vladya.

Geutier: Come along please.

Lenin: Fer-om to-day, n-on-co-operation.

> *And as* **Geutier**, *smiling bleakly, approaches the spoon again:*

N-o!

Krupskaya *(flaring):* You are worse than a child! I would rather nurse a monkey!

Lenin: You would der-ive a monkey m-ad!

> *She storms out. Hiatus. Then* **Lenin**, *dark-faced but ashamed opens his mouth wide.* **Geutier** *administers the medicine.*

Geutier: It isn't her fault Vladimir Ilyich. It is a Politburo ruling. As you perfectly well know.

Lenin: She put them up to it.

Geutier: It is largely owing to your wife that you're allowed to work at all. Did you know that?

Lenin: N-o.

Geutier: Well it is so. I would have you in hospital.

Lenin: You are a not-orious counter-rev-olution'ry ass-assin.

> **Geutier** *has been taking his pulse and now, angrily:*

Geutier: Oh look now, this is very bad. What have you been doing?

Lenin: N-othing.

Geutier *(suspicious):* Then what are you thinking of doing?

> **Kollontai** *and* **Lenin** *shifty. Then:*

Lenin: N-othing.

> **Geutier** *sniffs and consults with himself, then, snapping shut his bag, he sits with it on his knees and in a tone of patient reiteration:*

Geutier: Esteemed and indispensable Vladimir Ilyich. If you excite yourself beyond a certain point you will probably suffer another stroke. And if you suffer another stroke it will either reduce you to the status of a vegetable or if you are fortunate, kill you on the spot. So, whatever Madame Kollontai has come to talk to you about I trust you will use a little of your legendary determination to behave a little less like a retarded child, and a little more like a responsible adult. Good day to you both. *(He goes)*

Lenin: Now— *(He breaks off. To* **Chekist***)*

G-o away.

> *The man begins to go but then, embarrassed.*

Chekist: Comrade Lenin, my instructions w—

Lenin: G-o!

      Chekist *goes.*

Now. What has Ser-talin been doing, in Georgia?

Kollontai: I don't know what to do.

Lenin: What?

Kollontai: You heard what Doctor Geutier said.

Lenin: F-f-uck Do-o-o-o-!

Kollontai: All right! . . . Vladya, I will tell you everything I know if you will promise to keep calm.

Lenin: B-argain. Wh-at has he been doing?

Kollontai: He's been doing the job you gave him Vladya. He has purged the Georgian Party.

Lenin: He is p-uking on the Party! *Isn't* he?

Kollontai: Yes. The Georgean Central Committee have torn up their Party cards. And . . .

Lenin: Hmp?

Kollontai: Several Georgean Comrades have *(shrugs)* disappeared.

      He looks away absorbing this. Looks at her sharp and appraising. Then:

Lenin: *He* must d-isappear.

Kollontai *(startled):* What?

Lenin: No n-o. Att-ttack him at Congress. Vote him out. S-end him to M-ongolia!

Kollontai: Me?

Lenin: Who else have you got?

Kollontai: Tomsky, Rykov; no-one who could tackle Stalin.

Lenin *(sniffs, pauses then):* Ter-otsky could.

Kollontai: Yes, Trotsky could.

Lenin: Ser-talin is the Bonaparte! Get rid of him Alexia! You must!

      She still looks dubious.

What's the m-atter?

Kollontai: Vladya, two-thirds of the Delegates to Congress will be Stalin's nominees.

Lenin: Yes I know.

      He looks over his shoulder, grins a little.

So I have written a speech for Ter-otsky to deliver to them, in m-y name.

He produces a fat envelope with some satisfaction.

It will b-low C-omrade Stalin ther-ough the roof, in fer-agments.

Kollontai *as before.*

Now what's the matter?

Kollontai: If he delivers it in your name, aren't you afraid he will step into your shoes?

He thinks it over, then, a genuine question?

Lenin: Would they fit him?

Kollontai: No.

Lenin: Then he w-on't be able to, will he?

He looks away and smiles a bit, musing.

He wouldn't want second-hand shoes, anyway . . . Ter-otsky's shoes are made to m-easure . . .

He comes back to her.

Get it to him somehow. Tell him what I've said. You'd better go now.

Kollontai: Good bye my dear.

He nods, absently, very tired. But as she is going he says, appropos she doesn't know what, as offering an extentuating circumstance for something:

Lenin: History is devilishly hard you know.

Kollontai: What?

Lenin: D-on't hold Ker-onstadt against Leon Da-vidovich.

She hovers uncertainly a moment and goes. His head sinks; he is sleeping. But rouses to say to the empty stage:

It had to be d-one . . .

He sleeps again. Light change to moonlight. An owl hoots. He rouses and calls:

Nadya!

Chekist *enters.*

Chekist: Comrade?

Lenin: G-o aw-ay!

Chekist *goes.* **Lenin** *gestures angrily after him.*

G-o right a-way!

Owl hoots. He purses his lips and imitates the call. No response. He tries again, half-heartedly. Nothing.

Krupskaya *enters with a lamp.*

Krupskaya: What you you doing?

Lenin: There is an owl.

> *He tries again. No response. Then she does it, softly and seductively; the owl responds.*

There are two owls. Mine is deaf.

> *The* **Chekist** *walks across the back of the stage.* **Lenin** *angrily:*

If I see you a-gain I will re-port you to your su-mp-mp-periors!

> *The man disappears.* **Lenin** *watches him, breathing hard. Then:*

Lenin: Do you remember a document I gave you to put in the safe?

Krupskaya: Yes?

Lenin: Is it still there?

Krupskaya: Yes.

> *He grunts, but:*

Lenin: Are you sure?

Krupskaya: Yes. What am I to do with it?

Lenin: Open it, when I am dead. *(Restless and irritable)* Wh-at's the time?

Krupskaya: Ten past. Are you expecting to hear from Congress?

Lenin: Mm. Ter-otsky is going to ser-laughter Comrade Ser-talin.

Krupskaya: Vladya, Doctor Geutier said that if Congress proceedings were likely to excite you, you ought not to have them.

Lenin: Oh yes?

> *She is puzzled by his equanimity.*

Krupskaya: So we shall not be hearing.

Lenin: Sh-all.

Krupskaya: Vladya, no arrangements have been made for you to hear.

Lenin: M-ade my own arr-rrangements.

> *She glares at him, tries to turn to her work. But:*

Krupskaya: Do you think that you are made of iron?

Lenin: No.

Krupskaya: Perhaps you think I am.

Lenin: Yes.

Krupskaya: Well I'm not!

Suddenly she is weeping. Clumsily he thrusts his handkerchief at her. She almost snatches it, and dries her eyes.

Lenin: It's been hard on you, h-asn't-it?

Krupskaya: 'It'?

Lenin: We had a goo-ood ti-me in Siberia. D-idn't we?

Krupskaya: It was all right.

Lenin: F-unny sort of honey-moon.

Krupskaya: You only married me for company.

Lenin: Not true. N'eeded a secretary. *(He looks away)* Had Martov for company.

Krupskaya: Yes.

He hears the hesitation. Looks at her.

Lenin: They say that he is dying too.

Krupskaya: Vladya, he's dead.

Lenin: Martov?

Krupskaya: Yes.

He looks away again. She looks at him.

D'you remember Pyotr?

Lenin: Mm? No.

Krupskaya: You do. He bit the policeman.

Lenin: Oh! The dog. Yes, I remember Pyotr. He was a bit petty-bourgeois.

Krupskaya: He was a thorough-going proletarian.

Lenin: I knew him b-etter than you. He was petty-bourgeois.

Krupskaya: He bit the policeman.

Lenin: Yes. But he felt awful about it afterwards . . .

Krupskaya: Did he?

Lenin: . . . Yes . . .

She looks at him sadly. He registers her attention. Crisp and firm:

Petty-bourgeois.

Driver *comes in with a big brown envelope.*

Krupskaya: You can give that to me, Victor.

Lenin: Me.

Driver *gives him the envelope and goes. He gets it open but can't read what's inside. She holds out her hand for it. Suspiciously he hands it to her. She opens it, takes* *out a wad of typescript, hesitates. He points at it.*

Lenin: Ter-otsky.

Krupskaya: Vladya—

Lenin: R-ead!

Krupskaya: Vladya, Leon Davidovich isn't there.

Lenin: What?

Krupskaya: He's very ill; he's been sent to the South.

Lenin: Not there?

Krupskaya: No Vladya.

Lenin *(softly):* Oh, the foo-ool . . . The *fo-ool* . . .

Krupskaya: Vladya, he's ill.

Lenin *(shakes his head):* No . . . No . . . Oh the fool . . .

He looks at the papers in her hand, desolate. Points and says:

Ser-talin.

Reluctantly she turns over the pages.

Krupskaya: Vladya, Stalin's not a monster. Stalin is a horse. Don't you remember; we used to call him the horse?

Lenin: Read.

Krupskaya: 'Light Industry. Report by Comrade Zeyavich'.

Lenin: Ser-talin!

She leafs through the pages.

Lenin: What was that?

She turns back and affects to read.

Krupskaya: 'Komosol Finances. Report by Comrade Savarin'.

And turns on again. But he lunges for the papers and she snatches them from his reach.

Lenin: Nadya, which means more to you—? Me, or the Party?

Krupskaya: Oh, what a cruel question. *(Reproachful)* What would you say if I should ask you?

Lenin: The P-arty.

She lowers her head and reads:

Krupskaya: 'For the Organizational Bureau J. V. Stalin opened his report by regretting the absence of Comrade Lenin. Quote: Comrade Lenin regards Party Unity as the apple of his eye. It would rejoice his heart to be here. I have never seen a Conference so united and unanimous. Applause, the delegates standing. However there had lately been some talk within the Party of a Democratic Opposition. To what was

103

it opposed? It was opposed to the Party Leadership. A delegate: No, to the Party Machine.'

Lenin: Wh-o-?

Krupskaya: It just says 'a delegate'. 'Comrade Stalin wondered whether Conference should provide some elementary Marxist primer for the use of certain delegates. Laughter. He himself was not an intellectual but he had always understood that Marx believed in a material reality. Laughter. The comrade delegate would correct him if he was in error. Laughter. Or if Marx was in error. Laughter. But if Marx was not in error then the Party was not an idea existing in somebody's head, it was an actual institution, existing in reality; and in attacking its actual apparatus the comrade delegate was attacking the actual Party, for which he wished to substitute a mere idea of the Party or some actual party of his own. The Party would tolerate neither alternative. Applause. In the proletarian State there could be only one Party, because only one could represent the interests of the proletariat. What interest, Conference might wonder, did the Democratic Opposition wish to represent?'

Lenin: Sh-sh-it!

She looks at him anxiously.

Lenin: Go on.

She hesitates.

Nadya!

Krupskaya: 'The Comrade delegate was no doubt subjectively sincere. But as Comrade Lenin always stressed, a person might be revolutionary in his own esteem, and yet might play, objectively, a counter-revolutionary role. Comrade Lenin never shrank from the exposure of such persons, even in the Party, even indeed in the Party Leadership. He would follow that example. Nobody was indispensable. The Party alone was indispensable. He pledged his own unquestioning obedience to the actual existing Party; it was the Party of Lenin. Applause. The delegates and platform standing.'

Lenin: N-o.

He staggers to his feet, his chair falling. He reels away upstage. The **Chekist** *has appeared there.*

N-o-o! N-n-n-

He flails at the Chekist *with his stick, his breath guttering.*

N-N-N-!

He whirls and collapses into his arms.

Krupskaya: Vladya!

Blackout. Geutier *in spot.*

Geutier: The autopsy on Comrade Lenin revealed gross cerebral deterioration. The brain was found to be both structurally decomposed and greatly diminished in size. The source of Comrade Lenin's energy and will power in the closing stages of his life are medically inexplicable.

Light change reveals Stalin, Trotsky, Lunacharsky, Dzerzhinsky, Krupskaya, Kollontai, *seated.* Geutier *crosses, bows over* Krupskaya's *hand and:*

He was an amazing man.

She hardly responds. He goes; they stir and Lunacharsky *clears his throat. In unison they each take up two sheets of paper.*

Trotsky: May I lead?

They look at one another; no one responds. Then Stalin, *bitterly:*

Stalin: Who else?

Trotsky: I begin by asking if you all accept this document as Comrade Lenin's Will and Testament.

Krupskaya: It is his Will and Testament. He left it in my keeping.

Trotsky: Very well. I direct your attention to Paragraph Two.

Stalin: Naturally.

Trotsky: Will someone read it?

A hesitation, then:

Krupskaya *(reads):* Our enemies desire to see a split within our Party. Half the danger rises from the personal relationship between Trotsky and Stalin. Personally, Trotsky is without a doubt the most able man we have. But he is too self-confident.'

Trotsky: I do not think my personal abilities are critically important. Whatever confidence I have is vested in the Party.

Stalin: Bravo.

Trotsky: Please go on.

Krupskaya: 'Stalin, being General Secretary, has acquired enormous power. I question whether he will use it with sufficient caution.'

Trotsky: Comment?

Silence.

Very well then I will comment. The Party Secretary can't avoid enormous power. The Party has and must have dictatorial power. And we are not required to use our power with caution; we are required to use it with effect. Comrade Stalin has never failed to effect whatever task the Party gave him.

A stir, and:

Krupskaya: What are you doing?

Trotsky: I am doing to the best of my ability what I think Vladya would have done.

Krupskaya: 'Stalin is too brutal! This is not a trifle; or if it is, it is a trifle which may come to be decisively significant. He ought to be removed from office! And replaced by some more tolerant, loyal, courteous and considerate person'! That is what he *did*!

Trotsky: He was not at his best when he did it Nadezhda. Since when were tolerance and courtesy considered revolutionary virtues?

Krupskaya: And loyalty?

Trotsky: Personal or Party loyalty, Nadezhda?

She looks at him aghast, and away.

Comrades, if we had—as many of you think we have—a Bonaparte within our Party, now would be his moment. If we had a man so overweening in his self-esteem that he would like to step into the shoes of V. I. Lenin, now would be his moment. If we had a man so squalidly ambitious and so lacking in a proper pride that he would sell his revolutionary birthright for a mess of personal pottage now would be his moment. Such a man could seize this moment I assure you without difficulty . . .!

He has soared to the heights of his own imaginings, impelled by indignation. He lets it sink in and then, dramatically calm:

Happily there is no such man amongst us. It seems to me

this document invites the very thing it fears: the fragmentation of the leadership and faction in the Party. And though it is the work of the greatest Marxist of our day it is also the work of an afflicted man. Remembering this, and that it is our enemies who wish us split, I move that Comrade Stalin should remain in office, and this document should be suppressed.

Dzerzhinsky: Second.

Stalin: May I speak?

Trotsky: Of course.

Stalin: He says that I am brutal. Comrades, I was brutally brought up. I have never claimed to be a revolutionary from the goodness of my heart. Revolution is a brutal business. And the revolution here is far from carried through. I tell you that because I'd rather you got rid of me than stay on false pretences. I thank Comrade Trotsky for his selfless intervention. And submit to your decision.

Trotsky: I put my motion to the vote.

Dzerzhinsky: Aye.

Lunacharsky: Aye.

Kollontai: . . . Abstain.

Trotsky: Nadezhda.

Krupskaya: Oh God, I wish he were alive . . .

Dzerzhinsky: We all wish that.

Krupskaya *(whispers):* Aye . . .

Trotsky: Carried.

> *They all rise, quietly, gathering their things and going.* **Stalin** *crosses to* **Trotsky** *and thrusts out his hand.* **Trotsky** *takes it without enthusiasm but firmly, making a commitment.* **Lunacharsky** *and* **Trotsky** *left alone.*

Lunacharsky: That was generous, Leon Davidovich.

Trotsky: Generous?

Lunacharsky: Very.

Trotsky: What a likeable person you are, Anatole Vassilyevich . . . And how I despise you.

> *He goes.* **Lunacharsky** *left alone; the light fading.*

Lunacharsky: I remember wishing at the time that J. D. Trotsky had taken up the reins. It was only gradually that the revolutionary vigilance of Comrade Stalin revealed him for what he was. A life-long enemy of the working masses and objective agent of reaction . . .

He is standing in the single spot now, as at the beginning. He brightens:

But I should like to end on a lighter note. These anniversaries of Comrade Lenin's death are not, for those of us who knew him, altogether sad occasions. Comrades, we have been looking back. What, if anything, have we learned? Have we learned perhaps not to look back? The answer as we might expect is dialectical. The pull of the past is very strong, particularly in a man like me. Not just because my past was privileged. My parents were, as you might say, 'well-off' in moral matters too. Our servants always stayed with us. No, do not laugh—benevolence, however limited, is better than the other thing. And not a new invention. A medieval overlord if he could see today could say that he had exercised a cruelty comparatively limited and local. The Father of the Savage Tribe was after all a savage kind of father. Our animal progenitors, though red in tooth and claw, were naturally tender too. The nest of twigs, the hairy dug—oh what security! And there's the rub. For life is not secure. The pull of the past is the pull of death, the comfort and the darkness of the slime from which we crawled in scarcely differentiated forms, and the perfect peace of passive matter. You see, I cannot guess what cosmic irresponsibility may lurk beneath my sometime wish for gaslight in the library, my mother making music and my father speaking French . . . We Communists are rightly proud of our unique commitment to the Future.

He seems about to say something more. But then thinks better of it. And goes.

CURTAIN